Minstrels of the Dawn

Minstrels of the Dawn

The Folk-Protest Singer as a Cultural Hero

Jerome L. Rodnitzky

Nelson-Hall Chicago

Chapter 2 is a revised and expanded version of "The New Revivalism: American Protest Songs, 1945-1968," by J. Rodnitzky, *The South Atlantic Quarterly* 70 (Winter 1971), 13-21. Copyright © 1971 by Duke University Press.

Chapter 3 is a revised version of a Walter Prescott Webb Memorial Lecture, "Popular Music as a Radical Influence, 1945-1970," presented by J. Rodnitzky and published in *Essays on Radicalism in Contemporary America*, edited by Leon Borden Blair (Austin: University of Texas Press, 1972), pp. 3-31. Used with permission of the University of Texas Press.

Library of Congress Cataloging in Publication Data

Rodnitzky, Jerome L   1936-
    Minstrels of the dawn.

    Bibliography: p.
    Discography: p.
    Includes index.
    1. Protest songs—History and criticism.
2. Music and society. 3. United States—Popular culture. 4. Singers, American. I. Title. II. Title: Folk singer as a cultural hero.
ML3561.P6R6   784.4   76-4520
ISBN 0-88229-284-6

Manufactured in the United States of America

For Mother and Dad
who always saw a brighter dawn
for their children

Acknowledgments

I wish to express my gratitutde to a few individuals and groups instrumental in this book's completion. First, my special thanks to R. Serge Denisoff, editor of the journal *Popular Music and Society,* for generously sharing his own research and providing trenchant criticism and comments on aspects of my work. Denisoff has done more than anyone else to establish popular music as an area of scholarly activity. Although we continue to disagree on some points of interpretation, I have consistently benefited from both his encouragement and his frank and friendly criticism. My thanks also to colleagues in the History Department of the University of Texas at Arlington for their general commentary and suggestions. The research and final preparation of the book were greatly aided by modest but consistent grants from the University of Texas at Arlington's Organized Research Fund. I also appreciate Mrs. Michele Bock's skilled aid in typing the final manuscript. Finally, the book would not have been possible without the sustained help and encouragement of my wife, Shirley Reiger Rodnitzky, who read and typed all preliminary manuscript drafts.

Contents

PREFACE   ix

INTRODUCTION: Folk Music, Protest, and Cultural Heroes   xiii

PART ONE: THE FOLK-PROTEST MYSTIQUE   1

    1:   The Evolution of the American Protest Song   3

    2:   The New Revivalism: Protest Music as a Religious Experience   17

    3:   Converting the Masses: Popular Music as a Radical Influence   27

PART TWO: FOLK HEROES—LINKS ON THE CHAIN   41

    4:   Woody Guthrie: Father of the Now Generation   43

    5:   Phil Ochs: A Minstrel's Search for Martyrdom   63

    6:   Joan Baez: A Pacifist St. Joan   83

    7:   Bob Dylan: Beyond Left and Right   101

CODA: THE END OF AN ERA   135

    8:   The Day the Music Died   137

NOTES   153

SELECTED BIBLIOGRAPHY   169

SELECTED DISCOGRAPHY   181

Preface

The rationale for this book is the belief that folk-protest singers played an important role in the youthful political-culture revolution of the 1960s, and that protest songs were the most vivid symbols of an era that historians will no doubt label "an age of protest." Many factors contributed to the climate that made protest singers cultural heroes. In an era of idealism, the singers stood for ideals. To a younger generation moving away from materialism, folk music symbolized simplicity. For political activists committed to bringing power to the people, songs were a bridge to the youthful masses. Music was clearly the key ingredient. Never before in history had music meant so much to a generation. As rock performer Frank Zappa noted, many youths were loyal to neither "flag, country, or doctrine," but only to music.

Those committed to institutional reform increasingly saw that the struggle for change was more cultural and generational than political or economic. Many radicals suddenly turned their backs on the older generation and attempted to capture the young. Their hazy reform movement (often just called "the Movement") became a "countercultural" crusade and music was a logical cultural weapon. There was a good deal of talk about new alternate media to counter establishment views, but the new music and the phonograph records that disseminated it became the real alternate media, as opposed to vehicles like the underground press. If there was a counter culture, surely it lived between the microgrooves.

The protest music itself was often taken over by a burgeoning, ultra-profitable music industry, but it proved more difficult to compromise some of the singers and writers. A few artists were either financially independent enough or politically committed enough to remain social critics. Although they were only a small percentage of the music industry, they influenced a much wider group of fellow singers and writers. These protest singers often became cultural heroes for many American young people who could no longer find heroes in the traditional fields of politics, business, and sports. For the first time, musical artists were elevated to the status of statesmen and business tycoons. Musicians increasingly drew public attention during the twentieth century, but they were almost always depicted as glamourous entertainers with little social significance. Thus, the many recent books on American popular music in general and rock phenomena in particular tend to chronicle the growth of a fad and to treat the singers as mere celebrities. Some books show a praiseworthy desire to place music in a wider social context, but few authors have given the serious singers the thoughtful consideration they deserve.

This book examines the history of American folk-protest with particular stress on the evolution of the protest song, the protest singer, and the social forces that shaped the protest tradition during the twentieth century in general and the 1960s in particular. Throughout I have attempted to capture the flavor of folk-protest by centering on archetypical examples of singers, songs, and reactions to the music. The book has three major goals: to analyze the extent to which popular protest music has been a radical, politico-cultural influence since 1945; to describe how folk-protest was absorbed by popular music in the late 1960s; and finally to provide social and cultural portraits of four key writer-performers who became cultural heroes during the 1960s. In focusing on Woody Guthrie, Joan Baez, Phil Ochs, and Bob Dylan, I neglect some noteworthy protest singers like Pete Seeger and Tom Paxton, but I am convinced that the four artists selected were the seminal influences on contemporary protest music. Their personal appeal to elements of the youth culture can, I believe, tell us much that we need to know about the trauma of the 1960s and the malaise of contemporary youth.

Introduction:
Folk Music, Protest, and
Cultural Heroes

There is little agreement on what folk music is, and this haziness contributes to its mystique. One can ignore the problem of definition by adopting Pete Seeger's lighthearted suggestion that "if folks sing them, then they are folksongs," but the puzzle persists. Folklorists might agree that folksongs are older songs, usually of unknown authorship, passed down by aural tradition in several versions, and changed and altered by a number of folk musicians. The problem, however, comes with the so-called folk-revival on American campuses in the late 1950s. Thereafter, a folksong could be any song that sounded as if it had been handed down from the past. Suddenly a song's subject matter and the performer's style became key folk criteria. Thus in 1964 music critic Gene Lees caustically wrote guidelines for the aspiring campus folksinger:

Trains are alway good in folk songs. Also hunger, lonesome-
ness, homelessness, the land (even if all you've ever seen of it is
Central Park), the open sky, long roads, being out of work, girl
friends who died, and what a drag the Establishment is. Jails
are very good, too—really *in* this year. ... . And of course, it is
requisite that you protest—against unfairness, injustice, and
that kind of stuff.[1]

During the early 1960s folk purists usually linked the
synthetic, pseudo-folksong with attempts to combine political protest and folk music in the contemporary protest song. In
1962, for example, critics Paul Nelson and John Panake
asserted that protest songs were "pretentious, portentous, and
ponderous," and that folk-protest writers were just political
hacks who "wouldn't recognize either folk music or folk style
if it were walking along beside them in a peace march."[2]
Nevertheless, on college campuses classic views of folk music
were obsolete. There, folk music was a little understood but
immensely meaningful concept that brought forth visions of a
more human past society and a possibly more humane future
society. Like Zen Buddhism and organic foods, folk music
swept the colleges as a hip fad. Indeed, since the 1930s folk
music had a close connection to the radical left in America
(especially communists and socialists),[3] and had increasingly
been taken seriously by folklore scholars as a guide to past
social mores. However, as Dick Reuss pointed out in 1965, the
public generally viewed folk scholarship as "little more than
a series of guitar workshops" carried on for radicals and
beatniks.[4]

Yet in their unsophisticated way, college students did
appreciate much of folk music's uniqueness. Broadly speaking, American popular music has consisted of three major
categories—folk music, topical music, and Tin Pan Alley
songs for the mass media. Classical American music and jazz
have had important effects on all musical genres, but have
attracted relatively small audiences. Folk music was music
made by and for the masses—songs to be sung at home, by
yourself, and on the job. Topical music consisted of songs
that related news, had a specific message, or supported a

contemporary goal. The colonial broadside ballads, sung in
taverns by minstrels, represented the earliest American topical tradition. Political election songs represented another
type of broadside, and union-organizing songs still another
variety. The latest topical music consists of the many so-
called protest songs that refer, subtly or directly, to specific
social problems. Tin Pan Alley songs came into their own at
the turn of this century, when there was a mass urban
audience for sheet music and piano-based family singing.
Shortly thereafter, the phonograph, radio, and eventually hi-
fidelity further secured their future. The problem is that all
three musical genres have increasingly merged together so
that they are often indistinguishable. We now have topical
songs written in a folk style, changed through the folk
process, and disseminated through the mass media. Yet this
tendency toward amalgamation is a common twentieth-
century American phenomenon—a process that historian
Daniel Boorstin calls attenuation.[5]

Despite the blurring of distinctions, American youth
identified folksongs as ballads that told a story and focused
on the basic aspects of life. Moreover, folk music projected an
image of both honesty and community. The folksinger of the
past sang to and with members of his own community, and
although the folksinger of the 1960s generally sang to stran-
gers, he tried to create a feeling of shared intimacy. The stress
on frankness, honesty, and integrity was an important part of
the folk mystique. Genuine feelings that would have been
considered corny in the 1950s became more acceptable in a
period of moral reform highlighted by the civil rights movement. Thus in 1962 *Time* described folksinger Carolyn
Hester as a person who had "a gift for appearing as if she were
delivering the Truth every time she" sang.[6] And in 1964 a
Harvard undergraduate explained that he listened to folk
music because it was "honest," because it told the "truth,"
told "real stories about real life," and did not "mince
words."[7] Folk fans felt that the traditional songs had been
stripped of all pretense and phoniness by the passage of time,

and this image was quickly transferred to contemporary songs written in simple folk style. Purists might scoff that a Bob Dylan "folksong" bore the same relationship to genuine folk music as a Guy Lombardo number had to classical music, but the new songs were quickly given the seal of approval by such traditional folksingers as Pete Seeger. With a few polite bows to folk hero Woody Guthrie, in the form of blue jeans and simple dialect, the new folkies carried it off. For the college generation looking for something to venerate, these middle-class, urban guitar players became the living embodiment of the folk tradition. The argument as to what constituted folk music was, as usual, irrelevant. Folk music could be subdivided by historical era, category, and region, but it could not be defined. Folk music was clearly nonexclusive; it was available to all comers.

But why should folk-protest singers become American cultural heroes in the 1960s? In the early nineteenth century, American youths ordinarily found their heroes in politics—an Andrew Jackson, an Abraham Lincoln, or a Jefferson Davis. After the Civil War, heroes were more likely to be business tycoons like Andrew Carnegie and John D. Rockefeller. After 1900, with the rise of big-time sports, athletic stars were common cultural heroes. Home Run Baker generally replaced J. Pierpont Morgan in youth's affection. After 1920, as Daniel Boorstin and others have argued, heroes were increasingly replaced by celebrities. Boorstin defines a celebrity as someone who "is known for his well-knownness." Unlike the hero who is famous for his deeds, the celebrity is famous for his fame. Whereas the hero's reputation grows over the years, the passage of time destroys the celebrity. Indeed, the hero has by definition "stood the test of time." As Boorstin puts it, "The hero created himself; the celebrity is created by the media. The hero was a big man; the celebrity is a big name."[8] Celebrities did not really achieve fame through great deeds. Rather fame overtook them because of the demand for instant cultural heroes and the skill of one's press agent. Perhaps the classic celebrities are movie stars—from Mary

Pickford and Rudolph Valentino to Marilyn Monroe and James Dean.

Instead of posing heroes against celebrities, David Harris, a contemporary radical activist, compares heroes to idols. His analysis is invaluable in explaining the peculiar type of cultural heroes protest singers became. Harris saw idols and heroes as the two primary public figures. The idol "existed beyond the people" and provided a vicarious life. The idol taught people what they could not be, and thus they worshipped him or her as a "negation" of themselves. Marilyn Monroe, for example, was worshipped by people who knew that they could not be Marilyn Monroe. A hero, on the other hand, was "an available model" who taught people what they could be. The hero, according to Harris, was only the "embodiment" of human potential.[9] Although Harris was speaking primarily of the role he envisioned for himself and other lay, radical political leaders, his thesis surely applies to artist-activist types like folk-protest singers.

One factor which helped cast protest singers into the heroic mold was the increased pressure on all artists to be politically active and thus socially relevant. Traditionally, American artists had only to perceive the world through their singular artistic lens rather than interact with their environment. The exceptions, like Henry Thoreau, might choose to combine their art with model life-styles or acts of personal conscience, or like Harriet Beecher Stowe, Nathaniel Hawthorne, or James Fenimore Cooper, they might write subtle propagandist tracts, critical of society. The propagandist tradition was markedly enforced by the vogue for social realism in American literature after 1900 and more recently by the proletarian novels, paintings, and songs of the 1930s. However, the artist was seldom expected to enter the political or social struggle directly, for this would destroy his artistic detachment and perspective—that special ability to see and feel what the social grinds and political hacks could not. There is still a widespread feeling that writers must remain apart from society. An example is the theory that blacks and

Jews in America and the Irish in Britain often see their respective societies best, because they are not really in it and thus have an outsider's detachment.

Today fewer critics would argue the merits of artistic detachment. Such writers as Herman Melville, Jack London, and Ernest Hemingway had long made a fetish about writing from experience, but now even personal experience is often not considered relevant enough in an age of mass struggles. The long-standing charge that ivory-tower academics were irrelevant to our rapidly changing society finally has focused on artists, who have seldom been judged against standards of relevancy. In an age when traditional heroes were less often found in politics and industry, young Americans increasingly looked for those whose hearts were supposedly purer. Naturally enough they were often drawn to the young, colorful musical artists they admired. Thus an activist like Joan Baez, an abstract social-critic like Bob Dylan, or more general musical stars such as John Lennon and Janis Joplin might become cultural heroes. These singers often symbolized personal integrity, because youths felt that they lived according to personal ideals. Not only writers and singers, but actors too were affected by the new stress on activism. Each new presidential campaign has put more pressure on all artists to get involved personally as well as financially. During the 1972 presidential campaign, for example, George McGovern and Richard Nixon often could not outdraw Shirley McLaine or Charlton Heston. Jane Fonda's active antiwar career is another good example of the trend.

One interesting explanation of this artistic activism is Marshall McLuhan's subtle, confused media philosophy. If, as McLuhan insists, the medium is the message, then surely the song must be the singer, the painting the painter, and the book the writer. Whether McLuhan is right or not, we increasingly view the work of art through our image of the artist. And if McLuhan is right in viewing the artist as a kind of early warning system who senses social reality long before it becomes apparent to the multitudes, then anything the artist perceives may be worthy of serious consideration.

Certainly the most important factor behind the rise of the protest singer was the general activist climate that permeated collegiate culture in the 1960s. The quiet, lethargic generation that inhabited the campuses during Eisenhower's two presidential terms suddenly came to life with a vengeance. For artists and students alike, it was no longer enough to fiddle while Rome burned, and no longer sufficient to outline the dimensions of society's prison walls. The artist, especially, was encouraged to help put out the blazes, from the burning city ghettoes to Vietnam, and to help break all barriers to personal freedom. In the depressed 1930s, the activist artistic response was obviously fostered by social and economic crisis. In the prosperous but rootless 1960s participation was caused, in part, by the search for cultural heroes. The worst charge against an artist during the 1960s was that he copped out. Traditionally, one copped out by prostituting his art for fame or fortune. However, during the activist 1960s copping out often became indistinguishable from simply sitting out.

Most folk-protest singers walked a political tightrope by remaining on the fringes of the liberal establishment, while reaching out to the youthful campus-based New Left and the exuberant counter culture. In the 1930s Woody Guthrie had identified with the proletarian masses on a direct socialist basis, but in the 1960s Phil Ochs, Joan Baez, Bob Dylan, and other singers had hazier, more diverse, and more complicated political outlooks. Yet both Guthrie and the younger folksingers were good examples of what Christopher Lasch has labeled the "new radicalism"—a radicalism that merged power and art, attempted to raise an underground consciousness, exalted direct action, and sought to identify with the plight of society's downtrodden.[10] The folk-protest singers were clearly subversives, and in an era of paranoid governmental activity this bolstered their image as heroes. Yet, as intellectuals from Plato to Picasso have argued, art itself is subversive of the established order and artists are naturally antisocial. For if artists saw things from the common perspective, they would not create art. In America the 1960s furnished folksingers with a new activist perspective. Their response was to merge traditional folk styles and contemporary topical songs into what became known as the protest song. In the process they became true folk heroes of the era and turned the guitar into a political and counter-cultural weapon.

1 THE FOLK-PROTEST MYSTIQUE

"A folk song is a song that nobody ever wrote."
—*Author Unknown*

1: The Evolution of the American Protest Song

American music has seldom been a focus for social or political debate. Yet the 1960s witnessed a veritable revolution in American popular music, as protest songs and "message songs" of infinite variety competed for public attention. Like most revolutions, this phenomenon was less revolutionary than it appeared. Protest songs have always been with us, although there is a natural tendency to overlook their presence. Past trials are quickly forgotten, and yesterday's protest song becomes increasingly ludicrous and irrelevant. To survive, songs of discontent must communicate universal frustrations. Since topical songs are, by definition, custom-made for a particular time and place, they remain rigid period pieces. Thus there have been no real classics of American folk-protest. Diverse, local, and elusive, the protest songs of the past are nowhere because they were everywhere and sprang from a multitude of now irrelevant social settings.

Topical songs had an obvious appeal to pragmatic pioneers. Unlike sophisticated European symphonies and operas, they told a simple story and vented simple emotions. From the beginning, Americans sang about politics, wars, heroes, badmen, and misery, but their style was overwhelmingly personal. In contrast to most twentieth-century protest songs, the earlier ballads lacked positive social goals. Perhaps the most subtle songs were the laments of Negro slaves which we loosely categorize as spirituals. Cut off from their natural culture, religion, and community, slaves developed the spiritual as a substitute for all three. Singing in the fields constituted an invisible church service. Spirituals lamented the present, affirmed faith in the future, and often poked fun at whites through subtle lyrics.[1]

American protest songs took a distinctly modern turn with the rise of the International Workers of the World. Better known as the Wobblies, the IWW was a militant labor group which first organized in Chicago in 1904 and included socialists, anarchists, and syndicalists. Their simple plan was ultimately to sign up every worker in a single union and then call a general strike to decide who was going to run the world—workers or bosses. While pursuing this goal, the Wobblies used every possible means to foster worker solidarity, including a wide variety of songs.

At first the IWW used classic songs of revolt such as "The Marseillaise" and "The Red Flag," which were printed on a four-page songcard. However, the old revolutionary songs contained too much ideology and not enough humor and idiom. For example, one song started out:

Arise then, arise then,
Ye men of the plow and the hammer,
Ye men of the helm and the lever,
And send forth to the four winds of the earth
Your new proclamation of freedom.[2]

To counteract this, new livelier songs written by Wobbly members Joe Hill and Ralph Chaplin were added to the songcard. Hill, whose real name was Joel Emanuel Hagglund, was by far the most creative IWW writer. Emigrating to the United States from Sweden in 1902, Hill worked as a general laborer and joined the IWW in 1908. Over the years he had adopted the spirit of class struggle. Convinced of the evils of wage slavery, he began to write new-style labor songs—direct, bawdy, and topical. Hill borrowed tunes, lyrics, and ideas and twisted all three into the Wobbly idiom. For example, he changed the popular "Casey Jones" ballad into a timely protest song by substituting the Southern Pacific Railroad for the Illinois Central line and turning Casey from a heroic engineer to a strike-breaking scab. Every part of the established order was fair game for Hill's satirical songs—from industry to churches. One song noted:

> Some time ago when Uncle Sam he had a war with Spain
> Many of the boys in blue were in the battle slain.
> Not all were killed by bullets, though, not by any means,
> The biggest part that died were killed by Armour's Pork and
>   Beans.

And another titled "The Preacher and the Slave" remarked:

> Long-haired preachers come out every night,
> Try to tell you what's wrong and what's right;
> But when asked about something to eat,
> They all answer with voices so sweet.
> You will eat, by and by,
> In that glorious land above the sky.
> Work and pray, live on hay,
> You'll get pie in the sky when you die.
> (That's a lie).[3]

Hill was executed by the State of Utah in 1915 for supposedly murdering a grocer. He quickly became a legend to many laborers and his songs found a welcome place in the IWW's "Little Red Songbook," first published in Spokane, Washington, in 1909. Richard Brazier, a member of the committee which published the original songbook, recalled that they wanted songs which would run the "gamut of emotions," songs "of anger and protest" that would call their oppressors to judgment along with the entire industrial profit system. These songs were to deal with every aspect of the workers' lives and "sow the seeds of discontent and rebellion." The committee members were sure that "the power of song" would "exalt the spirit of rebellion."[4] Thus, the music of "The Battle Hymn of the Republic" became the tune for Ralph Chaplin's "Solidarity Forever"—the Wobbly anthem. In a few years the songbook grew to a volume of fifty ballads. The books were handed out to new members along with their union cards, and on each red cover was inscribed the motto: "To Fan the Flames of Discontent." One verse of "Solidarity Forever" summed up the IWW message neatly:

> They have taken untold millions that they never toiled to earn.
> But without our brain and muscle not a single wheel can turn.
> We can break their haughty power; gain our freedom when we learn
> That the Union makes us strong.
> Solidarity forever
> Solidarity forever
> Solidarity forever
> For the Union makes us strong.[5]

When the IWW was discredited by its opposition to World War One, both protest songs and militant unionism languished during the prosperous, raucous 1920s. However, when the Depression hit in the 1930s, protest music and unions revived under the stimulus of hard times. An axiom of labor organization is that workers sing only under great stress, and not surprisingly during the 1930s new unions like the CIO and United Mine Workers sang on the picket lines. With the wave of union organizing drives during the mid-1930s, came a flood of protest parodies of popular tunes. For example, when the sit-down strikers took over the General Motors plant in Flint, Michigan, they sang the following lyrics to the melody of the contemporary hit song, "Goody, Goody":

> When we walked out on you,
>   we set you back on your heels,
> Goody, goody!
> So you lost some money and now
>   you know how it feels
> Goody, goody![6]

For many newly organized workers unionism was a joyous

event to be celebrated in song, as the gospel was affirmed in religious music. Indeed, several famous labor songs used the melodies of popular hymns.

However, militant unionism became irrelevant during the production crisis of World War Two. More importantly, the postwar confrontation with Russia drove radicals of every persuasion out of labor organizations, and these were generally the individuals who encouraged songs of dissent. Long-term prosperity and suburban living have long since made union protest songs passé. A few unions still have songbooks, but since only a small percentage of workers attend union meetings, except during strikes, songs are seldom sung. Except for some very recently organized groups, like farm workers, labor unions are no longer singing movements. In any case, the union protest-song tradition remained for any organized movement to draw on.

Moreover, the union song deeply influenced Woody Guthrie, the father of the contemporary protest ballad. Guthrie, a restless folksinger and periodic hobo from the Oklahoma dustbowl, roamed from coast to coast during the 1930s, writing as he traveled. His songs were traditional in style, but included a new dimension. Transcending personal plight, his ballads subtly captured the underprivileged other America he knew firsthand. His songs reflected both the failures and possibilities of the nation. Guthrie was partisan, bawdy, erratic, and perhaps a naive ideological captive of the American left, but his simple, powerful ballads somehow rang true and captured aspects of the nation's glory and shame. Whether singing about dustbowl misery, the union struggle, America's natural beauty, or the plight of migrant workers, his voice was affirmative. As Guthrie noted, he "made up songs telling what" he "thought was wrong and how to make it right, songs that said what everybody in the country was thinking."[7] Like Whitman, Woody celebrated the strength of the common man and proclaimed:

> I am out to sing songs that will prove to you that this is your world and that if it has hit you pretty hard and knocked you for a dozen loops, no matter how hard it's run you down or rolled over you, no matter what color, what size you are, how you are

built, I am out to sing the songs that make you take pride in yourself and in your work. And the songs that I sing are made up for the most part by all sorts of folks just about like you.[8]

Guthrie's optimism characteristically appears in the title of his autobiography, *Bound for Glory*. After the war the same optimistic outlook would fire the imagination of a new generation of topical songwriters who sought a new world. Oddly enough, at one point Guthrie was subsidized by the Federal government. In the spirit of the New Deal's Federal Arts Projects, the Bonneville Power Administration commissioned him to write some songs to celebrate and whip up enthusiasm for the Columbia River Project. The twenty-six songs he completed for Bonneville were among his best and included "Roll On Columbia Roll On" and a subtle song of the migrant worker titled, "Pastures of Plenty."

Just before the war, Guthrie settled in New York City. Together with a small group of rurally-oriented traditional folksingers he planted folk music in a liberal, urban setting. This cross-fertilization would produce the legion of urban folksingers whose repertory was a mixture of traditional folksongs and topical protest ditties. It would also connect the urban folksong movement to the political left. One early indication of the new mood was the Almanac Singers, a group which included Guthrie and his young protégé, Pete Seeger, a Harvard dropout. The Almanacs mixed traditional folksongs with leftist politics and were especially interested in singing at union rallies. Characteristically, they recorded an album of antiwar songs in 1940, but withdrew it when Germany attacked Russia in 1941. They then brought out a record urging America to enter the war, and soon Guthrie joined the merchant marine and Seeger the army.[9]

After the war, many enthusiasts felt that the country was ready for a folksong revival which would mushroom through the union movement. In 1946 Seeger and others founded an organization in New York named People's Songs which published a magazine of the same name. The periodical crusaded for civil rights, militant unionism, and peace with

Russia—both editorially and through topical songs; and the organization produced a film-strip guide called "Sing and Win." Some ballads like "Listen, Mr. Bilbo" ridiculed Southern segregationists such as Mississippi Senator Theodore Bilbo. Another song, "The Gol-dern Red," lampooned union-busting, segregation, and red-baiting all in one package. Three verses of the latter ballad immediately sum up the style and goals of People's Songs:

> The speed-up was terrific, and the pay was mighty small,
> So we organized a union one fine day
> I said "Boss you better talk, or we"ll have to take a walk"
> And here's the very words I heard him say—(and I quote)
>> Why you're nothing but a gol-dern red (agitator)
>> Why you're nothing but a gol-dern red.
>> If you're for the CIO, you're a stooge for Uncle Joe
>> ·
>> If you strike for higher wages, you've been reading Lenin's pages
>> Yes, you're nothing but a gol-dern red.
> I took a Negro brother out to get some hash with me.
> The waitress blushed and looked the other way,
> The owner said "Get out—we don't want your kind about,
> And you won't get served in here til Judgement Day" (Here it comes)
>> Why you're nothing but a gol-dern red (just like Lincoln)
>> Why you're nothing but a gol-dern red.
>> If you think a man's a man when his skin is black or tan
>> Then you're nothing but a gol-dern red.
> Here's the moral to my story; if you strike for higher pay
> If discrimination gets you good and mad ·
> If you get into a fight for insisting on our rights
> Then you're sure to be denounced for something bad (Guess what)
>> Why you're nothing but a gol-dern red (Great God)
>> Why you're nothing but a gol-dern red.[10]

Not surprisingly, People's Songs was ignored by the unions, who now sought a more conservative image, and given comfort by the radical left, who welcomed any support. In 1948 the organization threw its weight behind the Progressive Party candidate, Henry Wallace, even to the extent of publishing a *Wallace for President Songbook*. In its brief two-year history, it became involved in enough dubious left-wing ventures to ruin the reputation of a hundred organizations. People's Songs did not directly ally itself with radical groups, but its willingness to sing for, and sympathize with, groups like the American Labor Party, the Progressive Party, and the American Communist Party made radicalism and folk music almost synonymous. One anticommunist joke of that era depicted two party members planning a meeting: "You bring the Negro," said one, "I'll bring the folk singer."[11] Above all, these writer-performers were turning out protest songs which topically attacked a broad spectrum of alleged injustices, from "civil rights" to "free speech." When People's Songs was investigated by Congress, the periodical called for songs to abolish the House Committee on Un-American Activities and to "militate action against an impending fascism which would mean death for all freedom in music." The editor concluded: "Let's get some brand new songs; let's rewrite some bold new ones: let's hit it from every angle with slams at the un-Americans and their activities, new exposés of red-baiting and anything else we can think of. But let's start turning them out and sing them so loud that they'll hear us in Washington."[12]

Embraced by the far left and deserted by the unions, People's Songs folded early in 1949 with patriotic groups snapping at its heels. The remnant of these protest writers went underground during the 1950s, although a new magazine, *Sing Out!*, gave them a means of national identity and communication. It appeared that the shortlived, urban topical-song movement had collapsed and been buried in its own activist, radical debris. During this period, many of America's leading folksingers were investigated by Congress and blacklisted by the media.

Counterattack, an organization committed to purging America's mass media of radicals in general and communists in particular, had since 1947 attempted to blacklist singers by publishing their associations with alleged subversive groups. Counterattack was especially effective in the early 1950s, during the McCarthy era's red scare. Its newsletter, also named *Counterattack*, and its bible, a slim volume titled *Red Channels: The Report of Communist Influence in Radio and Television*, became standard reference works for media executives.[13] Accordingly, even when folk music became popular in the 1960s, older performers like Pete Seeger continued to be blacklisted. Indeed, not until McCarthyism's decline and the rise of Martin Luther King's civil rights movement did protest songs re-enter mass culture.

People's Songs had completely failed to rally America into one great union through song, but it did produce scores of ballads that became models for the protest songs of the 1960s. Moreover, People's Songs symbolized the faith that solidarity and communication through music could generate social action. That optimism is still the most striking difference between the earlier protest writers and today's more cynical younger artists. The close connection to the unions probably oversimplified the struggle for the older writers. Their solution was always to join ranks, sing, and bring about reform by the growing weight of numbers. In 1963, Theo Bikel appeared at a civil rights rally along with many veteran singers and noted that they had come to signify their "conviction that not a single one of us will ever be free until we all are."[15] Similarly, in 1969 Pete Seeger reaffirmed his optimism by denying that politics was "the art of the possible." Rather, Seeger insisted: "The real art of politics is to make what appears to be impossible, possible."[15] This earlier optimism about the prospects for organization and solidarity would quickly break down during the complex 1960s. The youth culture was not interested in organizing, but in freeing itself from organizational restraints. Increasingly the writer-performers were neither optimistic nor pessimistic, but rather existential in their outlook. In an age of generation gaps, an obvious gulf developed between the earlier protest singers and their musical heirs. A primary cause was the tendency of younger writers to base their songs on secondary perceptions of society—usually from mass media. For older singers like Seeger, songs were weapons to be used in a struggle they had already joined. In contrast, younger protest singers tended simply to catalogue social ills without taking part in their cure. These subtle changes in outlook evolved between 1955 and 1965—a period which saw a steady rise in the popularity of topical, radical music. Yet commercial success left its mark and would completely change protest music's form, goals, and style.

The cultural isolation of the early 1950s gave folksingers the opportunity to reflect, redefine their philosophy and goals, and polish their arts. Imperceptibly, the focus changed from visions of a brave new world to a stress on the folk traditions of the past. Obviously protest songs were an integral part of these traditions and linking them to the American heritage bestowed a more wholesome image. In this guise, folksingers quietly invaded the musical vacuum on college campuses in the late 1950s. While jazz had become increasingly complex and abstract, rock-and-roll had steadily become more nonsensical and meaningless. The folk ballad, however, was extremely communicative and intelligible. Moreover, high school kids who were swept off their feet by rock-and-roll in the 1950s were ready for something more sophisticated and meaningful when they entered college at the end of the decade, and folk music took over by default.

Indicative of folk music's new success were the Weavers—a quartet of People's Songs performers—led by Pete Seeger. Though they were blacklisted by radio and television, the Weavers sang to packed audiences at college concerts and their records were campus hits. As the Weavers opened the breach, new folk recording artists and small record companies began reaching for the college market and a new wave of folk composition resulted. The Weavers, and especially Seeger, had popularized the earthy ballads of Woody Guthrie, now incurably ill and in the first stages of a hereditary disease that would eventually take his life in the fall of 1967. Guthrie had always been a defender of the oppressed, but above all he had been a restless man of the open road. He served as a striking bohemian model. Rejecting the security of their affluent backgrounds, many student folk fans identified with the Guthrie tradition and adopted hobolike life-styles.

Then suddenly in the late 1950s and early 1960s came the cataclysmic events that called folk guitarists to arms. Along with the student-led Southern civil rights movement came a variety of protest songs. Northern songwriters picked up the spirit and spun out a mass of polemics against racism, the arms race, and middle-class conformity. Commercial record companies quickly sensed the drift. Pleasant melodic groups like the Kingston Trio cashed in on the new college rage and popularized the movement even further. As the commercial success increased, the protest characteristics of the movement were diluted, but topical protest ballads continued to supply the most vivid picture of the folk craze. For example, in 1961 *Newsweek* reported:

> Basically the schools and students that support causes support folk music. Find a campus that breeds Freedom Riders, anti-Birch demonstrators, and anti-bomb societies, and you'll find a folk group. The connection is not fortuitous.[16]

The so-called folk protesters or folkniks were generally not ideological, but they were willing to associate with radical movements, even at the risk of endangering their professional future. Always present was the example of Negro students in the South. Media coverage of the sit-in movement gave vivid proof that Martin Luther King's passive resistance program was a sing-in movement as well as a sit-in movement. As King became the leader and "We Shall Overcome" the anthem of the civil rights struggle, Northern folksingers developed leaders and anthems of their own. While black Southern demonstrators wrote new songs and rewrote old ones to fit their specific campaigns, dynamic new Northern performer-composers like Bob Dylan and Phil Ochs pitched in with more general musical polemics against discrimination, the arms race, and the "military industrial establishment." Such gifted singers as Joan Baez and Judy Collins reached out for an ever wider audience. The syrupy, apolitical Kingston Trio was replaced by the more cynical and irreverent Chad Mitchell Trio and eventually by the aggressively liberal group Peter, Paul, and Mary. Such song titles as "Masters of War," "Talking World War III Blues," "I Ain't Marching Anymore," "Draft Dodger Rag," and "The Times They Are A-Changin'" immediately indicated what was on the minds of the new folk generation.

Yet if topical protest conquered the campus, it failed to dent the television media. As usual, the networks and sponsors were intent on avoiding controversy, and several folksingers, notably Pete Seeger, were barred from commercial programs in the 1960s. Seeger had been called before the House Un-American Activities Committee in 1955 and had invoked the First Amendment in refusing to testify about his past radical associations. Had he pleaded the Fifth Amendment, he could have escaped prosecution, but Seeger chose to argue that the guarantees of free speech and association granted by the First Amendment also guaranteed the right to remain silent about one's beliefs and associations. Seeger was prosecuted and, in 1961, finally convicted for contempt by a Federal District Court in New York City and sentenced to one year in prison. At his trial, Seeger pointed out that for twenty years he had sung songs for groups of Americans of every "possible political and religious opinion and persuasion" and had never refused a group because he disagreed with some of their ideas. He noted that some of his ancestors were religious dissenters who came to America over 300 years ago, and others were abolitionists in the 1840s. Seeger indicated his songs were in that tradition and asked the court for permission to sing a song in his defense, which the judge refused. Seeger appealed his conviction, and it was finally set aside in 1962 by the U.S. District Court of Appeals.[17] His exoneration, however, did not make Seeger more palatable to the media. In 1963 when the ABC network launched a television show called "Hootenanny," featuring top folksingers, Seeger, who had led hootenannies for years, was blacklisted. The more militant, and by this time the most popular, folk artists of the day rushed to Seeger's defense. Joan Baez, for example, dedicated a song to him at each of her concerts. Both Bob Dylan and Joan Baez, the king and queen of folk-protest, told "Hootenanny": no Seeger, no Dylan or Baez. Peter, Paul and Mary and other performers delivered the same message.

By 1965 the tide had turned. The merger of rock-and-roll with folk-oriented songs, which the entertainment industry christened "folk-rock," brought message songs to the high school crowd and the best-selling-record charts. One quickly recalls the media vogue for thoughtful songs like "Universal Soldier" and idiotic songs like "Eve of Destruction" which dominated popular disc-jockey shows. The so-called teeny-boppers were now dancing the newest frantic steps to pacifist and integrationist topical songs, electronically amplified by equally new and frantic rock groups. Message songs had arrived, and they seemed to be everywhere triumphant. But what kind of a triumph was it?

Back in 1961, during his darkest days, Seeger had depicted himself as a "cultural guerrilla" who operated within a cultural underground. He was taboo to the media, yet he could roam from campus to campus, sing a concert and move on. Above all, he prized college students, the "one sector . . . which refused most courageously to knuckle under to the witch hunters." Thus Seeger looked forward with confidence. He felt that the students who had learned his songs and style were "taking them to thousands of places where" he "could never expect to go." Though he could not get a job at a university, those whom he had helped motivate were now university faculty. Like fireflies these young people were to "light up the night," or perhaps imitate more aggressive insects. Seeger recalled that once a white politician had told Sojourner Truth, the nineteenth-century Negro abolitionist leader, "Woman, I care no more for you than a mosquito." "Mebbe so," said she. "But, praise God, I'll keep you scratching."[18]

Increasingly, however, it appeared that the topical song had been poisoned by its own success. As civil rights, antiwar, and student power movements spontaneously created their own songs, the guitar-strumming, singing demonstrator became a national stereotype. Once the stereotype was established, a host of commercial entertainers turned out scores of protest songs that were technically pleasing, general enough to attract various tastes, and above all, profitable. Originally growing out of a concrete social situation that called for redress, protest songs were now more likely an expression of an individual life-style. The most popular folk-rock songs of Bob Dylan, Paul Simon, and others had by 1966 evaporated into an existentialist haze. In attempting to be all things to all people, the compositions became do-it-yourself protest songs. One could read whatever one wanted into the lines. Stance became more important than goals. Whether or not the medium is always the message, the medium had obviously overtaken most protest ballads. However, although the song lyrics were increasingly hazy and thus less powerful, their influence was far more pervasive because of the simple weight of numbers and their matter-of-fact presentation. In any case, the tendency was to treat protest music as a life-style, divorced from actual goals. Our earliest protest songs have been forgotten because they were too diverse in origin, and are nowhere because they were everywhere. Ironically, many contemporary message songs probably will be quickly forgotten because by saying everything they in effect said nothing. Yet, perhaps there was something basically American in the contradiction and wild diversity of the recent protest songs. Bob Dylan, like Walt Whitman, might reply to critics: "Do I contradict myself? Very well then, I contradict myself. I am large; I contain multitudes."

2: The New Revivalism: Protest Music as a Religious Experience

Music has long been an integral part of religious revivalism in America. It is perhaps natural that in the 1960s protest songs became one cornerstone of a new secular revival. While the newer youthful movement retained the emotion, energy, and righteous anger of the older crusades, it utilized the focus of the social gospel. Whereas American revivalists from Jonathan Edwards to Billy Graham have castigated individual sinners, recent protest songs depicted a sinful society and exhorted the individual to redeem his community rather than himself. "You're a sinner," cried the old-style preacher and the chastened repentant replied, "Woe is me! I'm a sinful man," even though his remorse generally evaporated by the following Tuesday and seldom interfered with his evil ways. Nevertheless, the revivalist's words provoked a truly religious experience. Similarly, the recent protest balladeer warbled to his audience, "We're prejudiced" or "We're warmongers," and the crowd nodded in agreement, accepting a collective guilt for the nation. Although this mood may only have lasted until the record or concert was over, the residual effects were stronger and not easily calculated.

It is not capricious to compare a folk concert with a revival meeting, while the journey to a folk festival was probably as close as our society has come to a religious pilgrimage. The concert itself could produce the swaying and handclapping typical of old-time revivals, but it could also resemble the hush of a church service. Janis Ian, a young folksinger, recalled how strange she felt at her first Joan Baez concert when spectators stared her down for humming along. And in 1968 Roger McGuinn, leader of a folk-rock group, The Byrds, suggested that concerts were "like a ritual, almost religious thing" in which entertainers functioned spiritually as "the new clergy," whereas the traditional clergy had "lost their following by blowing a bad set."[1] In any case, folk gatherings generated shared emotion and a communal critique of society. Earlier the message was in the lyrics, more recently it often came via the music, but in either case the revivalistic flavor remained.

Critics of folk protest would no doubt label the "new revivalism" the new propaganda. Protest songs are easily viewed as the editorials, instruments, and weapons of an alien ideology—all the more potent because of their innocuousness and general appeal. For example, in 1966, Reverend David Noebel of the Christian Crusade did not agree with Francis Bacon that "generally, music feedeth the disposition of the spirit which it findeth." On the contrary, he seemed obsessed with Alexander Pope's observation: "What will a child learn sooner than a song?" In a long, overdocumented book, *Rhythm, Riots, and Revolution*, and a short pamphlet, *Communism, Hypnotism, and the Beatles*, Noebel charged that protest songs in particular and folk-and-rock music in general were part of a Communist plot to subvert America's youth.[2] Although Noebel's specific charges leaned toward the ridiculous, as a frightened professional patriot, he was one of the few individuals besides folk performers themselves who seemed to grasp the immense persuasive power of the musical idiom. Singers were seldom modest about their influence. In 1964 Peter Yarrow of Peter, Paul, and Mary claimed that his trio could "mobilize the youth of America . . . in a way that nobody else could," perhaps even sway an election by traveling with a presidential candidate. He added, however, that they were not going to use this power. It was enough to know that they had it.[3] In 1967, Timothy Leary, a former Harvard psychologist and vigorous advocate of psychedelics and hard-rock music, was equally extravagant in his claims, noting:

> The stereophonic machine plus psychedelics (and throw in an acid-light show for good measure) provides an instrument for evangelic education and propaganda that few people over the age of 30 comprehend.[4]

Yet those who now view music as a powerful weapon have long been anticipated. Jeremy Collier, a seventeenth-century Englishman, argued that music was "almost as dangerous as gunpowder" and might require "looking after no less than the press."[5] Plato perhaps spoke more directly to present social fears in *The Republic.* Commenting on new styles of music, he warned that "any musical innovation is full of danger to the whole State, and ought to be prohibited." He further observed:

> The new style . . . imperceptibly penetrates into manners and customs; whence, issuing with greater force, it invades contracts between man and man, and . . . goes on to laws and constitutions, in utter recklessness, ending at last . . . by an overthrow of all rights, private as well as public.[6]

However, if the power of music had been suggested in the past, it had never enjoyed the technical possibilities and wide audience that recent mass media provided.

Pete Seeger symbolized the revivalist optimism of contemporary protest singers about the power of music. For example, in response to the suggestion that songs are not worth beans as an influence on history, Seeger related the following story:

> A big steel cargo ship carried a full load of soy beans. There was a leak in the boat, but the captain didn't know about it. Every day when they checked the bilge, it was dry. The water

was being absorbed by the beans as it leaked out. One day that ship just split in half and sank. The beans had gradually swelled and swelled, until the pressure was too much; the steel plates cracked, just like that. Snap.[7]

The heyday of message music, however, was the early 1960s. In 1962 the appearance of *Broadside,* a magazine devoted to topical songs, was symptomatic of this renaissance. *Sing Out!,* the other national folk periodical, also drifted away from traditional music toward topical material. The period from 1960 to 1963 was the formative one. In these years Bob Dylan, Phil Ochs, Tom Paxton, Joan Baez, and Judy Collins picked up the mantle of Woody Guthrie and carried protest songs to new heights of popularity and power.[8]

Political lyrics were suddenly a musical vogue and part of the atmosphere. Roger McGuinn, who had never been aware of class suffering, found that he was "trying to get a political message into almost everything" he wrote, simply because there was a "left-wing thing" in the air.[9] The new stress on lyrics affected all popular music. A decade earlier recording companies consciously made songs a little unintelligible so that listeners could not easily memorize them from the radio. By 1962, however, lyrics that stressed equality became the focus of hit songs like Bob Dylan's "Blowin' in the Wind," and Pete Seeger's "If I Had A Hammer." The civil rights message reflected the influence of Martin Luther King's movement, but after 1965 pacifist and anti-Vietnam songs easily fit into the same crusading style. It is surely no accident that the most universal protest song of the era, "We Shall Overcome," was a reworked nineteenth-century revival hymn. And no more graphic picture of the folk-protest movement could be given than that of concert performers ending the evening by singing "We Shall Overcome" with the audience.

The success of topical music also brought a flood of poorly written songs that substituted slogan for art. One verse of a ballad printed in *Broadside* entitled "Modern Mother Goose" related that Old Mother Hubbard had left her cupboard to join a peace march, since the threat of nuclear weapons had convinced her that all eating might soon be terminated. And in one stanza of a song titled "Limp" a daughter assured her mother that although she and a fellow protest marcher were expecting an illegitimate baby, if the peace movement succeeded, at least the child would not have to march like his parents.[10] After 1965, however, it was increasingly recognized that politics was no substitute for musical technique or poetic imagination.

One important change in protest songs resulted from catering to the tastes of the high school crowd. The younger kids, nourished on rock-and-roll in the 1950s, were used to heavy music. Eager to please, record companies merged the high school and college markets by developing folk-rock; and soon teenagers were dancing to pacifist and integrationist tunes with a big beat. Throughout the 1960s folk-rock became heavier and more electric and those who supported it as high-schoolers remained faithful as collegians. By 1966 amplified protest music was everywhere triumphant and even traditional singers were turning in their acoustical guitars for electronic gear.

As the psychedelic revolution went on, the mood song replaced the message song. Increasingly, the music radiated general alienation and a hazy, nonconformist aura and content, as opposed to focusing on specific social evils. Perhaps this was inevitable, for as rock-and-roll sought to capitalize on the popularity of protest, it became profitable to be against something, or anything, or best of all—everything. The revivalistic flavor was still there; if anything the frenzy had increased, but the words were now unimportant, and anyway, they could seldom be heard over the music. Folk-rock said in effect, "Don't listen to what I say, watch what I do, or more accurately the way I do it." There is no doubt that psychedelic music registered protest, but it was a protest of form rather than substance. The music itself was sexual, highly creative, nonconformist, and clearly outside the idiom of white middle-class America. As Simon Kunen, a student radical, saw his hair as a symbol of protest, so might many a musician say of his music:

> But as for bad vibrations emanating from my follicles [music] I
> say great. I want the cops to sneer and the old ladies swear and
> the businessmen worry. I want everyone to see me and say:
> "There goes an enemy of the state," because that's where I'm at,
> as we say in the Revolution biz.[11]

Moreover, that was often the way it was with protest music.
Songs often had to portray their anti-Establishment credentials with the right slogans and a suitably loud volume, while
the performer had to adopt a suitably weird life-style. Ric
Masten's talking blues song, "The Protest Biz," made the
point succinctly:

> Got a call the other day, got a buzz from Sodom
> Down near Mickey Mouse land.
> Man says: I hear ya got songs baby? Protest songs 'bout peace
>   and labor strikes, freedom songs of civil rights.
> An' I said: Yes it's true. An' he says: Cool, baby cool!
> Says: I think you're a damn fool
> But I never let politics stand between me and money.
> I'm gonna make us both a bundle sweetie!
> I think you're a pink fink
> But that's the way it is in the protest biz!
> Said: I want ya to sign on the dotted line sweetie
> I want ya to point your finger for me at thirty-three and a
>   third.
> I'll put your picture
> All psychedelic and like that on the record jacket,
> With your big guitar and your long hair hangin' down.
> But I'm going bald, I said.
> An' he said: Oh I'm sorry, I must have the wrong number.
> But I got a beard, says I. Groovy! says he,
> I think you're a damn red an' I wish you were dead
> But like I said:
> That's the way it is in the protest biz.
> Are you interested? I said: no, I don't think so.
> He said: Now don't blow your cool sweetheart!
> Whatcha writin' them songs for?
> Ya want to reach the people, dontcha?
> Well come to me baby, if ya got a message,
> Not Western Union.
> Who do you think you're reachin' singin' to the walls like
>   that?
> Come to me baby and be heard.

I'll make ya rich and famous
Ya dirty Commie!
But that's the way it is in the protest biz.
Well I think it's a lousy way to make a buck, I said.
Now, don't point your finger at me babe!
Like where would you be without war and Watts and poverty.
Without labor strikes and tragedy,
You'd be out of business sweetie, with nothin' to sing about!
Beautiful, I said, I'll sing about faith, hope and charity.
It won't sell man! he said.
And I said: Mister . . .
And he said: Call me sweetheart!
So I said: Sweetheart. An' he said: Yeah?
And I said: Go to hell!
And he said: Well, that's the way it is in the protest biz.
And then he hung up.[12]

Jazz lost many of its adherents because it became too intellectual. Folk-rock, however, became increasingly anti-intellectual. The new stress on the sensory effect of the music rather than the verbal message was one aspect of an increasing belief that truth must be felt rather than rationally grasped. Whereas Woody Guthrie and Pete Seeger often deliberately played below their instrumental ability so that the musical background would not detract from the lyrics, folk-rock artists feared that the words might get in the way of the music. Words, after all, can mean many things, and some critics argued that since the music was the experience, the words could be artificial barriers between the individual and reality.[13]

The increasingly existential focus of folk-rock was an obvious threat to the effectiveness of protest songs, but the tendency of individual folksingers to cut topical songs from their repertory was a more pernicious development. The continuation of *Broadside* magazine, the 1969 publication of *The Vietnam Songbook,* and the continued success of Pete Seeger and Phil Ochs were sure signs that topical music was far from dead at the decade's end, but the decreased response clearly showed that it had been pushed to the fringes of the folk-song movement.

Like so many folk music trends, the movement away from topical songs was started by Bob Dylan, the most creative and influential performer of the 1960s. Dylan had started out to emulate Woody Guthrie and his early, overt protest songs like "Blowin' in the Wind," "Masters of War," and "The Times They Are A-Changin' " earned him the adoration of the political left. Dylan, however, felt his creativity had become captive to ideology, and in 1965 he declared his independence. Thereafter, his songs were intensely personal, hazy statements, with electronically amplified musical arrangements. He made his new philosophy crystal clear in a remarkable song titled, "My Back Pages." In this ballad, Dylan proclaimed that he had over-simplified right and wrong in his earlier songs and become what he hated most—a preacher. One line noted that he had deluded himself into believing that "liberty was just equality in school." However, at the end of each verse Dylan explained that he was "much older then" but "younger than that now." At the 1965 Newport Folk Festival, Dylan had performed with electric guitar and was loudly booed, while Pete Seeger was wildly cheered. However, Dylan had his revenge. Slowly but surely folk music followed his lead. Quite possibly Dylan was fleeing a world which sought to use him as a symbol. For while attempting to bring the masses into a confrontation with, or at least an awareness of, the evils of society, protest writers like Dylan found themselves threatened by a new demanding establishment. The aware sympathetic minority creates a new threat to personal identity, and the artist may try to escape the mob by looking inward at his own world rather than outward at theirs. Dylan no doubt believed that the mere act of protest denied the aesthetic and thus denied art. However, Phil Ochs, a leading topical writer, took vigorous exception. Like Dylan, he admitted that the world was absurd and that no amount of work could ever change its absurdity. Yet Ochs insisted that the struggle against absurdity was its own reward. For Ochs, it was not enough to know that the world was absurd and to restrict himself to pointing out that fact, for this would be a case of perception leading to inaction. Ochs sought perception leading to involvement, and he remained a vigorous revivalist, warning of moral damnation and the "fire next time."[14]

Perhaps Woody Guthrie, the artistic sire of folk protest, had the real answer to topical music's critics and dropouts. Guthrie explained:

> I don't sing any songs that are not real. . . . I don't sing any silly or any jerky songs. I don't sing any songs of the playboys and the gals that get paid for hugging the mikes and wiggling their hips. I sing songs that people made up to help them to do more work, to get somewhere in this old world. . . . I don't sing any songs about the nine divorces of some millionaire playgal or the ten wives of some screwball. I've just not got the time to sing those kind of songs and I wouldn't sing them if they paid me ten thousand dollars a week. I sing the songs of the people that do all of the little jobs and the mean and dirty hard work in the world and of their wants and their hopes and their plans for a decent life.[15]

Woody Guthrie simply believed that songs could be used to get all the good things people wanted. He had the true revivalist's faith that to see or hear evil was to hate it, and thus his job was to sing about what he saw. Characteristically Guthrie noted, "Let me be known as the man who told you something you already know."[16] Unfortunately the songs that Guthrie clearly meant to encourage social change sometimes became sublimations for involvement. It was too easy for folk fans to delude themselves into thinking that they were changing an evil world, when all they were doing was listening to records, strumming guitars, and attending concerts.

Nevertheless, the protest song movement was symptomatic of a dramatic change in the social awareness of the younger generation. The results of the new revivalism are still impossible to assess, but the modern American protest song may yet turn out to be the most dramatic symbol of a postwar era some historians will label "The Age of Protest."

3: Converting the Masses: Popular Music as a Radical Influence

"Ah, but in such a time of ugliness the true
protest is beauty."
—*From the Phil Ochs songbook,* The War Is Over *(1968)*

To talk of "radical influence" in contemporary America invites visions of stealthy conspirators, drugged fanatics, and wild-eyed terrorists. Indeed, during the 1960s many Americans insisted that what was most vivid must be representative. However, America's radical tradition could not be erased by emotion nor overwhelmed by headlines. That tradition has a long, honorable history and its proponents, from Roger Williams to Henry Thoreau to David Harris, have a prominent place among American folk-heroes. American radicals have always been preoccupied with fundamental reform, and dictionaries frequently define "radical" in terms of its Latin primitive *(radix,* root), as an adjective signifying reform that goes to "the root or origin" of a problem.[1]

Our past radicals usually confronted society with its seamiest aspects, and often demanded immediate changes through direct action. This has always upset many Americans and tended to make radicals unpopular. Like the proverbial messenger with bad news, the radical seldom received an enthusiastic reception. Yet those who disturb people are not necessarily radicals. Blowing up buildings does not make one radical, nor does proclaiming revolution, nor needless to say does taking drugs or hair-length qualify you. The radical is characterized by visions of a future society and by rational plans to bring his dreams to fulfillment. In youth's idiom a radical is not merely turned off; he must be turned on to alternatives.[2]

Yet within this classic intellectual tradition important new trends emerged. Historically, the conservative right celebrated the social status quo, while the radical left sought new alternatives. In twentieth-century America, this usually meant concerted efforts to preserve the capitalist system against socialist onslaughts. However, since 1945 the divisions between left and right have steadily blurred, as both sides became more dissatisfied. The right continued to attack society as decadent and proto-socialist, while the left began to criticize welfare state bureaucracy and demand "participatory democracy," a trend no doubt fostered by the intellectual dominance of so-called "liberalism" in our media and universities. As "New Deal" liberalism grew quantitatively, it often declined qualitatively and constituted a loose ideological shelter for many defenders of the status quo. Inevitably radicals rejected the old political boundaries and moved into the ideological vacuum from both sides. It is no accident that Ayn Rand's conservative objectivists see themselves as radicals. Increasingly, diverse groups profoundly disturbed by society seek a radical identity. For example, a California-based evangelical group calls itself "The Christian World Liberation Front" and is proud to have its missionaries called "Radicals for Jesus" or even "Jesus Freaks."[3]

While American radicalism has undergone this recent transformation, popular music has played an important role in the development of a radical mentality, especially among youth. Indeed, the most important changes in contemporary message music are its pervasiveness, technological vividness, and ability to influence the youthful masses. Another new development was the new music's often frank political agitation. Agitation can be simply defined as "persistent urging of a political or social question before the public"; and what better way to reach the public—especially the young public—than on the proverbial "wings of song"? Did not Henry Thoreau label music "the arch-reformer"? Little wonder that in 1968 Frank Zappa, lead singer of The Mothers of Invention, asserted that music could help engineer a painless revolution, rather than a "blood in the street" uprising, by perfecting advertising techniques that Madison Avenue used to sell washing machines. Zappa expected to use "the system against itself to purge itself" and argued that his music was "constructive" since it supplied "therapeutic shock waves."[4] Putting aside these grandiose claims for the movement, it is likely that even now no group of writers, teachers, or preachers can rival songwriters in communicating with youth. In the case of folk-rock music, the message communicated was often difficult to perceive because of the general clownish atmosphere that has always pervaded rock music.

Yet it is naive to pass off the influence of rock music by poking fun at its commercial trappings—clothes, ridiculous group names, and zany antics. The diverse, illogical, sensory nature of rock music may have been quite appropriate for youth in general and radical youth in particular during the 1960s. As songwriter Malvina Reynolds suggested in 1967, American youth were "word sick," for they had "been talked at, lectured at," and commercially propagandized until "they believe nothing and are influenced by everything."[5] Rock singer Country Joe McDonald indicated that really grasping the total reality of Vietnam would probably have driven him insane. Answering his own question as to what you do about it, Country Joe replied, "You take drugs, you turn up the music very loud, you dance around, you build yourself a fantasy world where everything's beautiful."[6] However, McDonald's group, Country Joe and the Fish, also mixed antiwar songs, like "Fixin' to Die Rag," in with their psychedelic escape music. Indeed, hard rock sometimes met the absurdity of the world by overwhelming distasteful reality with an existential world of personal emotion.

There was no direct link between psychedelic dropouts and political terrorists, yet both groups discarded rational dialogue and lived in an alienated world which either completely rejected or embraced ideology. It was not surprising that when the Rolling Stones, a British rock quartet, first came to the West Coast, a small, violent splinter group issued a proclamation of welcome which noted:

> Greeting and welcome Rolling Stones, our comrades in the desperate battle against the maniacs who hold power. The Revolutionary youth of the world hears your music and is inspired to even more deadly acts. . . .
>
> We will play your music in rock-n-roll marching bands as we tear down the jails and free the prisoners, as we tear down the State schools and free the students. . . .[8]

The Rolling Stones were nonpolitical and definitely uninterested in overthrowing capitalism. However, the Stones too scorned rational discourse, and their song lyrics were hazy enough to be perceived as radical hymns. Their "Street Fightin' Man," a best-selling record which said nothing about political upheaval, was often seen as a revolutionary marching song because of its title and fervor.

If the Stones were not opposed to capitalism, it was at least their business to appear antiestablishment. Here is where radical activists and psychedelic dropouts came together at the bandstand or jukebox. Youthful alienation was primarily based on the belief that impersonal powers controlled one's life, and there were two classic responses— either drop out or fight the machine.[8] Often both dropouts and activists saw themselves as radical reformers. The activist sought to change the world while the dropout's dissent was a personal negation of society. The radical activist generally patronized the dropout, but was willing to view rejection of society as a possible first step toward political action. Most younger radicals had given up on the American worker as a reform vehicle and turned to a wider cultural approach which saw youth as a revolutionary class. Thus, radicals had increasingly adopted C. Wright Mills's view that the new struggle was not between classes but between the "power elite" and the masses. The power elite controlled the media; and hence the radical cultural effort strove to reach the young before they could be programmed. Popular music now became a major political weapon, since the new radicalism was primarily a youth movement. The cliché, "Don't trust anyone over thirty," was one tired example. Perhaps it is less clear that the prime pacifist theme pervading psychedelic music, "Make love not war," was hardly directed at the older generation.[9]

Precisely because radicals found it so difficult to confront their adversary in our complex corporate society, the new political battleground became largely cultural and generational rather than social and economic. This new struggle had been popularized as "The Making of a Counter Culture."[10] The idea was to reject and destroy the old culture in order to liberate the individual. While some saw this as a negative, destructive act, many radicals insisted that it was a positive move which forced critical evaluation of society. In this regard popular music could sometimes be a vehicle for cultural fragmentation.[11]

Ironically, music's vast power to influence was sensed by the often ludicrous professional anticommunist groups long before the issue of a counter culture arose. In 1965 Reverend David Noebel of Tulsa, Oklahoma's fiercely fundamentalist and anticommunist Christian Crusade sounded the alarm. In his two amazing books, Noebel thoroughly accepted Pete Seeger's comment that "the guitar could be mightier than the bomb."[12] Noebel concluded that communists had infiltrated and subverted American folk-and-rock music to hypnotically brainwash American youth with Marxist ideology. As far as Noebel was concerned, "the noise" that millions of youth called music was "invigorating, vulgarizing, and orgiastic." While destroying youth's "ability to relax, reflect, study, and meditate," it in fact prepared them "for riot, civil disobedience, and revolution." Noebel viewed the marriage of rock and folk music as "a total capitulation on the part of the U.S.

record companies to the Red-infested folk field."[13] He warned that this synthesis "could well spell the doom of" America, since no nation could "long endure with its younger generation singing itself into defeatism, pessimism, a peace-at-any-price mentality, disarmament, appeasement, surrender, fear of death, hatred toward the South, atheism, immorality and negation of patriotism." For Noebel the effectiveness of the "Marxist folksingers" in making their listeners "feel nauseated at living in America" was illustrated by the "togetherness of . . . folksingers and student rioters" and also by teenagers "screaming in Beatle concerts."[14] In 1965 Noebel's work seemed typical of the communist-conspiracy syndrome. Today, in the midst of a cultural war for the allegiance of the young, Noebel's analysis seems somewhat less ludicrous, once divorced from the paranoid issue of communist subversion.

Much of psychedelic music does project a hypnotic mood rather than a message. Yet, though the lyrics are not explicit, the music has an indirect radical influence by showing contempt for social mores in areas such as sexual behavior, obscenity, and drug use. Also, since cultural changes are often more shocking than calls for fundamental social reform, radical political positions may look harmless by comparison. Drug songs, for example, were often more distasteful to the radio audience than political songs and by 1969 they became a public issue. In December 1969 television personality Art Linkletter asserted that half of the most popular records were "concerned with secret messages to teenagers to drop out, turn on, and groove with chemicals." And in September 1970 Vice-President Agnew charged that much of "rock music glorified drug usage."[15] Indeed many radio stations had long banned overt drug songs, but they often overlooked the lyrical double meanings of songs like Bob Dylan's hazy, mystic, "Mr. Tambourine Man," and John Lennon's "Lucy in the Sky with Diamonds." However, it was natural for drugs to be a topic of rock music, since the songs reflected the world of youth and singers. Whether or not the young took them, drugs were a definite part of their culture, just as alcohol is an important ingredient of the adult world. Drinking is commonly mentioned in the lyrics of dozens of old adult standards. However, those who insisted that psychedelic music had specific cultural or political messages were deluded. Its major quality was an existential stress. Folk-rock influenced by rejecting social control and allowing one to read almost anything into the lyrics. The music represented a life-style, and while it could help induce political radicalism, it destroyed specific political protest. By being all things to all men, it inevitably became meaningless at the social level.[16]

One writer logically divided classic protest songs into magnetic and rhetorical types. While the former songs aimed at building group solidarity and adding members to the movement, the latter sought to pinpoint specific conditions that called for redress.[17] But folk-rock songs did not fit in either category. They called not for solidarity but for diversity; they did not point out specific social ills, they depicted general absurdity. Whereas the older protest songs made radicals feel better, they usually did not make many converts. The listeners were convinced in advance. Popular music with vague protest themes made some converts subtly. Youths first attracted by the music, often later imbibed the style and finally perhaps read something of personal significance into the lyrics. By the late 1960s, even serious establishment organizations sometimes tried to get their ideas across through rock music. For example, in 1970 the Campus Crusade for Christ sent a folk-rock group called Armageddon from campus to campus in an avowed effort "to change the world." The advertising flyer they distributed to students jauntily announced that Armageddon had:

> . . . a sound that competes with the top in pop and a message that tops the top. . . . Judge for yourself. Allow Armageddon's electrical sound to massage your ears and rap with your mind.[18]

From religious appeals (including folk masses) to commercial and even political advertising, music as communication was everywhere triumphant. The question was not its use, but its immediate and long-term effects—especially on the new generation. Mankind has a long sad history of noticing the revolutionary effects of new technology too late. We still know little about what happens to a generation brought up on television or even about the social effects of the telephone. We know less about the influence of message songs. Some suggest that song lyrics may have a subliminal effect and act as a catalyst for alienation and/or political action. Others insist that protest songs usually serve as a symbolic substitute for personal involvement. After all, it is perhaps too easy to feel that you are moving society when all you are doing is listening to records or singing along.

Yet, if the new popular music did not induce overt radical action, it could produce a new kind of togetherness that bordered on the hypnotic. Singing in groups or listening alone, one feels bold. Thoreau noted, "When I hear music, I fear no danger. I am invulnerable. I see no foe. I am related to the earliest times, and to the latest." Similarly, singing protest marchers were often charged with a communal euphoria, which could constitute the emotional highlight of their dissent. For example, in 1969 a University of Wisconsin coed criticized *Newsweek* for concentrating on the few violent incidents in a campus demonstration, while ignoring "the 10,000 peaceful marchers singing together by torchlight."[19] By torchlight, by daylight, on the march, or in the concert hall, there was a magic that can be sensed if not rationalized. Perhaps the charisma came across best in the key line of the Paul McCartney-John Lennon song, "The Word": "Say the word and be like me. Say the word and you'll be free."[20] The word was, of course, LOVE, but at a given rally the magic word could have been freedom or peace.

Increasingly the charisma, hypnotism, and euphoria were big business and in terms of the youth market, very profitable. This did not alarm some reformers. For example, Simon Kunen felt that capitalism had "a self-destruct mechanism." Kunen argued that the corporate media only sought profit and if radical, revolutionary materials were profitable, corporations disseminated radicalism and revolution.[21] Most radicals are far more pessimistic and feel that the mass media co-opt radicalism by diluting its content and dulling its fervor. For example, when protest songs were accompanied by a full orchestra, art was improved but the message and ardor suffered. Likewise, when President Lyndon Johnson proclaimed "We Shall Overcome," the song and slogan lost much of its meaning. And while the pacifist ballad "Universal Soldier" became a nationwide hit, the Vietnamese war accelerated. More ironically, Glen Campbell, who recorded "Universal Soldier," supported the war and was quoted as saying that "anyone who wouldn't fight for his country was no real man."[22] Many radicals have rejected commercial music as a reform vehicle. By 1969, Irwin Silber, former editor of *Sing Out!*, concluded that popular music's "cultural revolution" was a threat to radical reform. He argued that the American working class instinctually sensed that electronic folk-rock was "basically a middle class trip." Although Silber believed the youthful alienation reflected by the new music was a chief symptom of capitalist society's disintegration, he also felt that doing your own thing was a "bourgeois trait" that capitalism was based on. Silber charged that "groovy life styles" suggested that workers ignore the system that oppressed them rather than fight to change it.[23]

Commercialism could just as easily destroy protest music by subverting the performer as by diluting content. Many former protest singers have cut topical songs from their repertory, either to increase their earnings or because they tired of musical agitation. Indeed, a number of successful younger songwriters such as Leonard Cohen, Joni Mitchell, and Tim Hardin forsook social subjects for deeply personal themes written in abstract poetic form.

At the same time, since music is only a tool, songs may become a conservative or even racist force. The left has perpetuated the myth that protest songs are, by definition, humanitarian attacks against the status quo. Historically this has not always been the case. For example, the Ku Klux Klan used songs to further their movement. Thus, "The

Klansman's Jubilee," sung to the tune of "The Battle Hymn of the Republic," noted:

> We rally 'round Old Glory in our robes of spotless white;
> While the fiery cross is burning, in the silent silv'ry night.
> Come join our glorious army in the cause of God and Right,
> The Klan is marching on . . .[24]

Another example is a 1961 song parody called "Kosher Christmas," which was published in *Thunderbolt*, the periodical of the National States Rights Party. In part, the lyrics proclaimed:

> Out of the East came three wise men,
> Levy, Goldberg, and Uncle Ben.
> The Christians all spend for Xmas Day
> And Goldberg will give six months to pay.
> . . . .
> Down the chimney old Santa comes
> With a bag of toys from Isaac Blums.
> Ring out the old, ring in the new
> While your money goes to some foxy Jew.[25]

The downtrodden poor may agree with Havelock Ellis that "if a man cannot sing as he carries his cross he had better drop it," but conservatives are more likely to paraphrase the revivalist and ask: "Why should the [radicals] have all the good tunes?" Indeed, the recent success of conservative and patriotic country-and-western songs like Merle Haggard's "The Fightin' Side of Me" and "Okie from Muskogee," as well as Guy Drake's "Welfare Cadillac," suggest that protest songs on the right may become a permanent feature of popular music, and that records may become an ideological battleground.[26]

Yet direct, serious protest songs are far from obsolete. They will probably never attain the commercial popularity they enjoyed in the early 1960s, but they remain a powerful American art form. Protest ballads still play a central role in America's major contemporary social struggles. The continued publication of *Broadside*, the dozens of antipollution and pacifist songs, and the recording of protest-song albums by women's liberation groups are ample evidence that musical ballads will continue to be a radical political force in the

1970s.[27] However, even when songs are used by very militant groups, they will doubtless remain peculiarly American. At a 1967 symposium in Cuba, Xuan Hong, a Viet Cong singer, defined a protest song as "militant in content, national in form and popular in idiom."[28] These criteria have little relation to American protest songs. Our most effective protest ballads have been subtle rather than militant, poetic rather than merely idiomatic, and their orientation has been universal rather than nationalistic. American protest music has invariably sought to make individuals feel guilty. As songwriter Buffy St. Marie noted, many Americans grow up believing that social problems are someone else's fault, and topical songs can dramatically suggest personal responsibility for social ills.[29]

The really serious protest singers have usually been on the fringes of mass culture, but their influence often grew geometrically through their effect on others. The small audiences they garnered were often activists who stimulated many others. Also, radical songwriters subtly influenced more popular fellow artists through artful, topical lyrics and their own personal, moral commitment. The medium may, as Marshall McLuhan insists, be the message, but this should not obscure the importance of messages within a medium. In our multi-medium culture there is a multiplier effect. Other media like films and television reinforce specific ideas that songs suggest. Films such as *M.A.S.H.* and *Catch-22* reinforced pacifist songs, and the graphic television coverage of the Vietnamese war and the resistance to it, stimulated both pacifism and the act of dissent.

The generational results were striking. In the 1950s relatively few college students were radicalized during their college years. Generally, not until they were juniors and seniors did they discover that American society has serious faults. However, in the late 1960s relatively large numbers of freshmen entered the university already dissatisfied with American society. As early as 1964, James Dennison, a Michigan State University administrator, complained, "These kids today are so darned serious they worry us."[30]

Popular protest music played an integral part in making numbers of youth more serious, radical, and politically worrisome. Yet, increasingly, protest music's influence became broader and harder to pinpoint. Young radicals and youth in general consistently stressed the desirability of personal choice and diversity. The goal was to renounce doctrine and exhibit a personal moral commitment. Inevitably, idealistic folk writer-performers became models for activist youth.

In an era still pervaded by fear of youthful dissent, contemporary observers are unlikely to assess the radical influence of popular music with any degree of detachment. Yet the pace of change is too rapid to wait until the dust settles and passions cool. Historians are well aware that outlandish past radicalisms have often become the fashionable reforms of the present, and that what was too much in one decade can be too little in the next. As Marshall McLuhan likes to put it, "Whoever discovered the water, it was probably not the fish." As for what cultural radicals loosely called "the movement," to some it seemed childish nonsense, to others a devilish conspiracy to destroy America, while to many of the radicals themselves it constituted a holy crusade. In any case, it was clear that many youths were seeking something our society lacked, and to some extent various forms of popular protest music spoke to their needs.

In 1968, social critic Paul Goodman lamented that America had no credible program of social reconstruction and sadly noted, "The young are honorable and see the problems, but they don't know anything because we have not taught them anything."[31] The same year Country Joe McDonald sensed "an incredible amount of energy coming out of the young kids"—from the "black ghetto . . . and a white hippie ghetto." He suggested that these forces were lying dormant and asserted, "If someone can come along and tell them which way to go or what to do, then I'd say maybe we got a revolution."[32]

However, Country Joe never said what kind of revolution; and protest music provided neither direction nor leadership. As Pete Seeger noted, songs after all "lie only halfway between thought and action" and unfortunately "may become a substitute for both."[33] Yet many of our affluent youth probably embraced protest songs because they lent meaning to their otherwise aimless, amoral lives, and because they salved their guilt and proclaimed their humanity and their fellowship with the oppressed. Our finest protest ballads may be regarded as both poetry and art. Perhaps it was President John F. Kennedy who best explained their true influence and value, when he observed:

> When power corrupts, poetry cleanses. For art establishes the basic human truth which must serve as the touchstone of our judgment. The highest duty of the writer, the composer, the artist is to remain true to himself, and let the chips fall where they may.[34]

Our best protest-song writers have indeed been a cleansing force. They have had the revivalist's faith that to hear of evil was to hate it. Their songs constituted a radical influence, but more importantly they supplied examples of conscience and principle to a society which has increasingly been unable to provide its young with credible examples of either conscience or principles.

2 FOLK HEROES – LINKS ON THE CHAIN

4: Woody Guthrie: Father of the Now Generation

> I hate a song that makes you think that you're not any good. I
> hate a song that makes you think that you are just born to lose.
> No good to nobody. No good for nothing. Because you are
> either too old or too young or too fat or too slim or too ugly or
> too this or too that. . . .[1] (Woody Guthrie)

Woody Guthrie was a complicated man and his life and
songs are filled with contradictions. However, the passage
above catches the basic theme that makes Guthrie a folk hero
to successive generations of rebels, bohemians, and defenders
of the oppressed. Whatever arguments rage about Guthrie's
personal ideas and motivations, few would deny that he loved
people and had an instinctual feel for the dignity of every
human being. Labeling Guthrie a socialist, communist,
radical, or folksinger misses his universal appeal. No contemporary black militant could read the passage above and
fail to see that Guthrie knew the importance of cultural

pride. No radical organizer could miss Guthrie's optimistic "can—do" faith in people's ability to control their destiny successfully. Black militant, woman liberationist, SDS member, labor organizer, student power advocate, Chicano, farmer, or hard hat—all would sense that Woody was one of theirs. Guthrie died in 1967, and his long losing struggle with Huntington's chorea (a progressive disease of the nervous system) had kept him confined to a hospital room since 1955, yet his spirit could be seen everywhere in the radical 1960s.

Woody Guthrie was born July 14, 1912, in Okemah, Oklahoma. It was to be a banner year for the Democratic Party, and Charles Guthrie named his second son and third child—Woodrow Wilson Guthrie—after the newly nominated Democratic standard-bearer. The Guthries were a vigorous but unlucky family. Woody's father was captive to Oklahoma's "boom-or-bust" psychology, and the family fortunes fluctuated with Charles's speculative real estate ventures. When Woody was two, the family moved into a new six-room house in Okemah's best neighborhood. Within two years the home burned to the ground and the family fortunes started on a downward path that they never recovered from. Woody's autobiography, *Bound For Glory,* is filled with his boyhood shock at suddenly having to settle for a lower standard of living and his father's shame at forcing his family to live below their accustomed style.[2] Considering Woody's eventual fervent proletarian outlook, it is ironic that his earthy, ex-boxer father was nonetheless by nature a rabid risk capitalist. Perhaps it was his personal experiences with the heartache of boom-and-bust spirals that turned Woody against capitalism and toward systems that offered economic security. Woody obviously grew up convinced that life was capricious and whatever it granted was easily taken away.

After retiring from real estate, Charles Guthrie took a succession of jobs that kept the family fairly comfortable, but the Guthries were soon struck with a series of personal tragedies. Clara, Woody's older sister, was killed by an oil stove explosion. Shortly thereafter, Woody's mother, Nora,

FAN THE FLAMES of DISCONTENT

SONGS

Cents   Printed in U.S.A.

Cover of the I.W.W. Songbook

Woody Guthrie, pictured below in his heyday, is considered one of America's greatest balladeers. Lower left is a later picture of Woody taken shortly before he died of Huntington's chorea.

Pete Seeger, left, sings to a crowd of 3,500 in United Nations Square, 1961. With Gil Turner, right, Seeger entertains at a peace protest sponsored by the New York Council of the National Committee for a Sane Nuclear Policy.

Pete Seeger as he appeared in 1970.

began to develop symptoms of Huntington's chorea—the inherited neurological disease that would eventually kill both her and Woody. A brief move to Oklahoma City in 1923 eventually brought a good job offer by Charles's brother-in-law, Leonard Tanner, but it quickly ended in disappointment. Leonard, a motorcycle dealer, was suddenly killed in a motor accident and Charles was once more unemployed. After the family's return to Okemah, tragedy struck again. Charles Guthrie was severely burned in yet another household fire, and he spent eighteen months recovering in Pampa, Texas, at his sister's wheat farm. Meanwhile Nora's nervous system had degenerated so badly that she was institutionalized at the State Asylum for the Insane.

Woody, then thirteen, moved in with his older brother Roy, and the two continued the haphazard, odd-job life that their father had recently led. These were formative years for Woody—attending high school and scratching around town for work. Moreover, they were a time of giddy independence and abject poverty. In effect Woody was a teenage hobo. He started by collecting junk and ended by polishing shoes and spittoons. Woody quit school in 1928. For a year he wandered around the Texas Gulf Coast—picking crops and doing odd jobs, before returning to Okemah. By the summer of 1929, his father had recovered enough to return to work and Woody joined him at Pampa. Woody had learned to play the harmonica in high school, and in Texas his uncle Jeff got him started on guitar. Regarding Pampa, Woody noted, "If there was anybody there that did not play some instrument I did not see them." Teaming up with Jeff, Woody soon "played for rodeos, centennials, carnivals . . . fairs" and assorted local celebrations.[3] He now began making "up new words to old tunes" to sing out his thoughts. As Woody put it:

> . . . there on the Texas plains right in the dead center of the dust bowl, with the oil boom over . . . and the hard-working people just stumbling about, bothered with mortgages, debts, bills, sickness, worries of every blowing kind, I seen there was plenty to make up songs about.[4]

After turning twenty-one, Woody married Mary Jennings, "a fine Irish girl," and they "lived in the ricketiest of the oil town shacks long enough to have no clothes, no money, no groceries and two children, both girls."[5] Meanwhile, Woody's mother had died in the State Asylum and his father married a mail-order bride. Woody was now mostly a sign-painter by profession, but as the Depression and dust storms steadily made Pampa an economic disaster area, he decided to seek his fortune in California. In 1937 he left his family, although he planned to send for them when he got settled and had saved some money.

There followed a five-year period of wandering around a depressed America for which Woody's recent life had thoroughly prepared him. The local hobo became a drifter on the national road. The closest place to home for Guthrie during this period was California. In Los Angeles, he and his cousin Jack sang on a fifteen-minute radio show. Woody then moved to Glendale, California, where he met Louise Crissman, "a tall thin-faced cornfed Missouri farmgirl" with a rough, husky voice. Billed as "Woody and Lefty Lou," they sang for two years on Radio Station KFVD in Los Angeles and briefly on a station in Tiajuana, Mexico. Guthrie then began singing on KFVD by himself, and shortly thereafter he sent for his wife and two daughters.

In 1939 Woody began writing a daily column for a communist newspaper, *People's Daily World*, while continuing his radio show. Here Woody became truly converted to militant unionism. While singing his own topical songs to a broad spectrum of city and farm workers, he picked up the ideologies of the steady stream of communist, socialist, and traditional labor leaders that drifted through California. Guthrie had become a radical minstrel of the workers. As he put it, "I always read the radical papers over my program and took sides with the workers all I knew how."[6]

Meanwhile, Guthrie met Will Geer, a leftist actor, and the two sang for striking migrant workers throughout California. At this time his first son, Bill Rogers Guthrie, was born. The struggling labor movement did not offer a way to make a living, so Guthrie took his family back to their shack in Pampa, and moved on alone to New York City to seek his fortune. In New York, Guthrie lived with Will Geer and his wife for a while, but soon moved to the poverty-stricken Bowery district. He then duplicated his California life-style— singing on radio shows and lending his support to a variety of radical causes in general and union activities in particular. His *People's World* column was now also carried by the *Daily Worker,* the official newspaper of America's Communist Party. Moreover, Guthrie recorded his first songs for posterity.

After meeting Alan Lomax, the folklorist and collector, Guthrie agreed to accompany him to Washington where Woody "recorded several hours of questions and answers and all of the songs [he] could remember on a pint of pretty cheap whiskey." These would become the famous Library of Congress recordings. Back in New York he recorded some "Dust Bowl Ballads" for RCA Victor, which were inspired by his viewing the film *The Grapes of Wrath* "three times in a row." Guthrie then met Pete Seeger, "a long tall string bean kid," and after working together on a songbook, they drove down through the South and Southwest together. In Oklahoma City, the pair stayed with Bob and Ina Wood, "the organizers of Oklahoma's Communist Party." Guthrie later wrote that the Woods had given him as good a feeling as he ever got from being around anybody in his entire life. They made him see why he "had to keep going around . . . making up songs." He had never known "that the human race was this big before," never known "that the fight had been going on so long and so bad." If Woody was tempted at this stage to make himself a commercial singing success, perhaps this southern swing dissuaded him.[7]

Guthrie brought his family to New York and continued his radio career. Soon tiring of the censorship imposed on his material, he headed south again, then westward to California. On the West Coast, the Federal government's Bonneville Power Administration invited him to write some songs commemorating the Columbia River Project in the North-west. Woody accepted. He wrote twenty-six songs that were used in the campaign to build public support for the project. After returning to New York, Guthrie joined Lee Hayes, Pete Seeger, and Millard Lampell to form a group known as the Almanac Singers. This quartet toured the country, specializing in singing at union halls and worker rallies. Back in New York, Guthrie began writing songs urging American intervention against Hitler after Germany attacked Russia. When America entered the war, the Almanacs sang on overseas broadcasts for the Office of War Information. Woody had recently been divorced by his wife and he finally joined the Merchant Marine. In 1942, before his first tour of duty, Guthrie married Marjorie Mazia Greenblatt, a New York actress and dancer. As a merchant seaman, Guthrie was involved in the Italian and African campaigns and his ship was twice torpedoed. Between sailings, Woody, Cisco Houston (another wandering folksinger) and Blind Sonny Terry (a black blues artist) recorded twelve albums of songs for Moe Asch, the founder of Folkway Records. Guthrie left the Merchant Marine in 1944 and remained in New York City, supporting the war in song. Ironically, on May 8, 1945, the day Germany surrendered, he was drafted by the army.[8]

After the war, Guthrie joined the People's Songs group in New York and ended up vigorously supporting Henry Wallace, the Progressive Party candidate for president in 1948. Other New York folksingers were making money now. The Weavers (a quartet that included Pete Seeger, Lee Hays, Ronnie Gilbert, and Fred Hellerman) were popular throughout the 1950s and had even made Guthrie's dust bowl song, "So Long, It's Been Good to Know You," a best seller. Yet, the commercial pace of folk music had already passed Woody by. After a few feeble attempts to catch up with the musical drift, Guthrie slipped back to his nomadic, bohemian life. In 1951, his new traveling companion was Jack Elliott, the dropout son of a New York physician. Elliott soon became the most successful Guthrie imitator until the emergence of Bob Dylan in the 1960s. Unfortunately, Guthrie's artistic life was tapering off, while his body was moving toward a tragic genetic fate.

In the early 1950s he suffered the first symptoms of Huntington's chorea: mental tantrums, depression, and loss of muscular control. By 1954 he was under constant medical supervision and by the next year he was confined to a hospital—a physical exile for the remainder of his life.

There is good reason for going into some detail on Guthrie's life. His art and outlook were pre-eminently the product of his life. His songs directly reflected his life experiences. Just as Thoreau worked out and lived out his ideas in the woods, Guthrie worked up his ballads on the road. Both Thoreau and Guthrie fit securely into the American pragmatic tradition. Both sought to drive life into a corner—to taste life at its bitterest or most sublime. However, Guthrie, unlike Thoreau, was never insular. Thoreau was rooted in the settled East. Guthrie's mind and travels embraced the entire continental United States. In the words of Woody's most famous song, from the "redwood forests" to the "Gulf Stream waters," the land was indeed Guthrie's. Woody was not unlike thousands of other rootless young Americans in the 1930s—traveling, but without a specific destination. It was natural for these young men to feel that anywhere was better than their sad, discouraged communities. It was easy for them to believe that out beyond their state lines there was a young vibrant America waiting to be discovered. But whereas thousands made Guthrie's journey, Woody was one of the few who wrote both constantly and passionately about his experiences. In his songs, newspaper columns, and homely prose, he was a sounding board for an inarticulate other America—used to hard times but stunned by the despair of depression. Today these people are usually called disadvantaged. In those days they called them poor, mistreated, and unemployed, and Guthrie had personally shared their fate.

Important, dramatic, and sweeping as Guthrie's life was, it is his legend and not his life that makes him the "Father of the Now Generation." Behind the postwar, protest song phenomenon was the dramatic rise of a new type of social agitator—the protest balladeer. Most of the contemporary folk writer-performers saw Guthrie as the seminal practitioner of the art. The successful writers of the 1960s demanded an authentic folk hero. They could hardly have worshipped the early commercial folk successes like the Kingston Trio or Burl Ives. Wobbly songwriter Joe Hill was too obscured by myth and too distant in time to be a flesh-and-blood idol. Guthrie was the logical choice. It is quite ironic that Woody never became famous until his illness forced him to retire as a writer. Only then could his more commercial imitators and worshippers elevate him to the status of historical father and make his name a household word.

Guthrie was easy to venerate since you could always interpret his life and ideas to suit any preference. Woody forcefully spoke against discrimination of any type. He declined to sing "any songs that make fun of your color, your race, . . . the shape of your stomach or the shape of your nose." Instead he sought to sing about people fighting "to win a world where you'll have a good job at union pay, and a right to speak up, to think, to have honest prices and honest wages and a nice clean place to live in and a good safe place to work in."[9] Hard-hat and college student, liberal and conservative, black and white, would likely say amen to those sentiments. Above all else, Guthrie had a universal outlook, and he felt his songs were a universal message in a universal language—music. As he vigorously proclaimed:

> Some people liked me, hated me, walked with me, walked over me, jeered me, cheered me, rooted me and hooted me, and before long I was invited in and booted out of every public place of entertainment. . . . But I decided that the songs was a music and language of all tongues.[10]

Woody's son Arlo relates that "Woody used to say that the worst thing is to cut yourself loose from people and the best thing is to sort of vaccinate yourself right into their bloodstreams." Arlo observes that when he was born, "Woody told the nurse to put down 'All' on my birth certificate where it says 'Religion.' They wouldn't do that so Woody told them it was either 'All' or 'None.' "[11]

If Guthrie's world view was universal, his political view was partisan. For Woody there was only one struggle—"the fight of the worker to win his fair share from his owner (boss, etc.)." To engage in this battle, any folksinger had "to turn his back on the bids of Broadway and Hollywood to buy him and his talents out." Woody was certain beyond doubt that he was on the side "that every child knows is the right side."[12] Like Walt Whitman, Guthrie saw himself as the voice of the inarticulate and powerless poor, or from the Marxist historical viewpoint, as an edge of the historical wave. He once explained his art in these explicit Whitmanesque terms:

> You may have been taught to call me by the name of a poet, but I am no more of a poet than you are. I am no more of a writer of songs than you are, no better singer. The only story that I have tried to write has been you. . . . You are the poet and your everyday talk is our best poem by our best poet. . . . I am nothing more nor less than a photographer without a camera. So let me call you the poet and you the singer, because you will read this with more song in your voice than I will.[13]

Ironically, Pete Seeger came across a comment in Guthrie's notebooks that warned, "I got a [sic] steer clear of Walt Whitman's swimmy waters."[14] The comment suggests that Guthrie drew heavily on Whitman's style and indeed Woody was more of a painter of uniquely personal visions than a taker of still photographs. Yet many performers see him as everyman. Country Joe McDonald prefaced his version of Guthrie's ballad, "This Land Is Your Land," by explaining that Woody "was just an ordinary man" who "made all the mistakes, had all the vices . . . that every ordinary person has. He never gave you the feeling that he was better than you" or "worse than you"; but that "he loved you because you were just like him and he was just like you." McDonald concluded that Guthrie "tapped the reality" of "what it meant to be an American."[15]

If Woody was ordinary, he had more than ordinary partisan political fervor. In 1948, at least, he was down on the Republican Party in general and Thomas Dewey in particular. Guthrie observed, "I have spent ten years thinking up reasons why I didn't like Herbert Hoover, and now I multiply by nine and I've got Dewey." Now the picture was clearer for Woody. The enemy was "out there in plain sight." The union men and voters had driven fascists and bosses "out of their ten thousand little hiding holes, and forced them, herded them, corralled them, all over into one big Republican Camp." Guthrie felt that "all of the fascist-lovers and Nazi-lovers" had "sent Dewey valentines on his day of nomination."[16]

Guthrie's various exaggerated political statements put him squarely in the radical camp, but his political image has been twisted beyond belief by those trying to depict him as a hip, modern radical. In 1967 Irwin Silber, an early organizer of People's Songs, wrote that you could not really understand Guthrie unless you understood "he was, in the most fundamental sense, a totally-committed, 24-hour revolutionary, determined to turn this whole world upside down." For Silber, Woody had a general outlook that "ultimately required the complete destruction of the world he knew." Silber observed that like Woody, Che Guevara "was some kind of nut," and asked if there were a Woody Guthrie somewhere "in this nightmare land we call the U.S.A." who could "write and sing the real Ballad of Che Guevara." Similarly, Silber asked if there was a Che Guevara somewhere "in this midnight" who could "raise his machine gun high above his head and inspire a people to take this land and make it their land."[17] Thus, Silber created an image of Guthrie the guerrilla fighter. After all, Woody did say this land was your land; he did inscribe on his guitar: "This Machine Kills Fascists." Yet somehow the picture of Woody and Che walking down the road, machinegun and guitar in their respective hands, strains the imagination. However, it is not surprising that Silber felt in 1966, during the Vietnam war, that it was obscene for the Secretary of the Interior to name "a dam or power station for Guthrie."[18]

The right also had an easy time seeing Guthrie's radical, pernicious side. In 1966 the Reverend David Noebel, a fierce anticommunist, complained that the image projected of

Guthrie was that he had written some "dust bowl songs, kid songs, union songs . . . a book called *Bound For Glory* and presumably went to Sunday School the rest of the time." Noebel asked: "What about the Woody Guthrie that wrote columns for the *People's World* and the *Daily Worker?*" Noebel's answer was that Guthrie had been significantly involved "in the communist subversion of American folk music." Noebel charged that Guthrie had been "identified under oath as having been a member of the Communist Party" and that his efforts in support of international communism were "well known."[19]

Between these two extremes of love and hate for Guthrie the revolutionary there is a whole range of tolerant admiration for Woody the displaced American and creative songwriter. For Pete Seeger, Guthrie was a symbol of honesty born out of "just plain orneriness." Seeger felt that Woody's self-image was like Popeye's: "I am what I am, and I ain't gonna change." Thus, Guthrie "was going to cuss" and was not "going to let New York make him slick and sleek and contented." This involved resisting the pressure to make him stop writing for the *Daily Worker* and losing a number of lucrative jobs. For Seeger, this was all part of Woody's remaining a "rebel until the end." Pete also learned style from Guthrie. He admired Woody's "ability to identify with the ordinary man and woman, speak their own language without using the fancy words and never be afraid—no matter where you were; just diving into some situation, trying it out."[20] Tom Paxton, a younger topical singer, learned a similar lesson. "Woody, above all, gave us courage," Paxton said. "He taught us that we can't run fast enough or far enough to stay out of trouble if we are going to be honest in our writing."[21] The conclusion was clear: to be an honest folksinger, Guthrie-style, was to be poor, and Woody surely met the test of poverty. It was his self-confessed followers—Dylan, Ochs, and Paxton—who had indicted themselves by their commercial success. The times really had changed when Bob Dylan could get rich singing "The Times They Are A-Changin'." If Guthrie had helped change the times, there was little evidence of his effect during his singing and writing career. Only after his forced retirement did his songs become widely known or his personage revered. His honored position was obviously a symptom of the folk revival and not one of its causes.

Guthrie's music is hard to classify since it covers so much ground. However, there are four main categories of song which were largely chronological in development—dust bowl songs, union songs, Federal government propaganda songs, and children's songs. The dust bowl ballads are represented by such songs as "Blowing Down That Old Dusty Road" and "So Long, It's Been Good to Know You," which tell of men driven from the land, and "Tom Joad," Woody's song about the hero of John Steinbeck's *The Grapes of Wrath*. These songs are simple and stark and their style lends them authenticity. "Pastures of Plenty," Guthrie's melodic hymn to the migrant farmworkers, bridges the gap between the dust bowl ballads and his union songs, while its allusions to America's physical beauty are a foretaste of his most famous song—"This Land is Your Land." The union songs run from quite specific songs like "The Union Maid," a tribute to union women, to much more abstract ballads that depict the plight of the poor in earthy parables. A good example of the latter is "Pretty Boy Floyd," which makes a Southwestern Depression-era bandit into a Robin Hood, and in which Guthrie testifies that he "never saw an outlaw drive a family from their home." Another such song is "Jesus Christ," which adapts the views of the more extreme social gospelists and turns Jesus into a radical organizer of the poor and a thorn in the side of the wealthy.

His Federal propaganda songs were largely ballads supporting New Deal projects, like the Bonneville Dam songs the government commissioned him to write. The best known of these is "Roll On Columbia." They also include songs urging on America's World War Two effort—ballads like "The Sinking of the Reuben James," "Dirty Overhalls," and "Round and Round Hitler's Grave." A large group of children's songs like "Grassey Grass Grass," "Riding in My Car," and "Why Oh Why" testify to Woody's love of children.[22]

Guthrie's songs do not lend themselves to simple verbal analysis, since his style was always more important than his message. His grainy voice, simple musical arrangements, crude musical accompaniments, understated lyrics, steady prolific output, and lack of commercial success all lent credibility to his work. He wrote about what he saw, but more importantly he composed songs for a purpose. He was one of the first Americans since the Wobbly writers really to believe in songs as a weapon in the class struggle. In the words of the title of a book of songs that includes many Guthrie composi- tions, Woody wrote *Hard Hitting Songs For Hard-Hit People*.[23] This was the truly heroic and historic aspect of his life. To play down Guthrie as a propagandist of the lower class and to center on his numerous individual strengths, weaknesses, and quirks is to lose his real significance.

However, for many Guthrie became a life-style model, divorced from his songs and his thought. Guthrie, the man of the people, became Guthrie the mod singer. Woody, the blood-and-guts union man, became Woody the existential hero. The hearts of the new folkniks were with Woody Guthrie, but their eyes and ears were open to Bob Dylan and Jack Elliott. Perhaps Paul Nelson, editor of the *Little Sandy Review*, caught the ridiculousness of the Guthrie-oriented folk scene best of all. Reporting on the 1962 Newport Folk Festival, Nelson observed:

> Gone were the sailors . . . in their places were the fraternity folklorists, the Bronx Baezes and Ramblin' Jack Somebodies . . . the stars-in-their-eyes worshippers. . . .
> Neophyte non-conformists, the young men were courte- ous, polite, affected in a sort of pseudo-Western manner, all dressed in blue or tan jeans, all trying hard to look, walk, talk, act in a way both highly humane and casually road-weary. The hair was erratic, the clothes as rumpled as parents would allow; the accent was drugstore cowboy, that non-regional dialect of the Shangri-La West that Bob Dylan and Jack Elliott hail from, that mythical nowhere where all men talk like Woody Guthrie and are recorded by Moses Asch.[24]

Bob Dylan's approach to Guthrie was typical of the adulation and emulation Woody received from aspiring folksingers in the 1960s. If Guthrie, like Dylan Thomas, had already died, perhaps Bob Dylan would have named himself Woody Zimmerman. Singers like Dylan borrowed other names and contented themselves with adopting Guthrie's style. That style included faded denim clothes, nomadic wandering, a colloquial rural-American dialect, and an identification with oppressed minority groups. More important, it included writing songs about things you had either experienced or had read about. Thus, to imitate Guthrie was eventually to become a topical singer.

From 1959 to 1961 Dylan became a self-created facsimile of Guthrie. He had liked Guthrie's songs earlier, but now he read Woody's autobiography, *Bound For Glory*, and discovered Guthrie the hard traveler. Dylan began to invent a hobo's heritage. He vaguely alluded to being from Oklahoma; he constantly stressed he had been drifting around the country almost all his life. More importantly he began to make Guthrie songs his specialty. According to one early acquaintance, Dylan "knew more Guthrie songs than Guthrie knew."[25] Finally, Dylan got to New York and visited Guthrie several times in 1961. He even sang his ballad, "A Song to Woody," to Guthrie.

Dylan's Guthrie phase had been run through a decade earlier by folksinger Jack Elliott. Elliott, whose real name was Elliott Adnopoz, was the son of a wealthy Brooklyn doctor. In 1951 he traveled around the country with Woody and picked up the whole spectrum of Guthrie mannerisms and the spirit of Woody's music. During the 1950s Adnopoz emerged as Ramblin' Jack Elliott and even as "the son of Woody Guthrie." Dylan met Elliott in New York and picked up some of Guthrie's style second hand. It was not entirely unfair to refer to Dylan at this time (as some observers did) as "the son of Jack Elliott and the grandson of Woody Guthrie."[26] It is equally true that whereas Arlo Guthrie was once known as Woody's son, now Woody is more likely to be described as Arlo's father.

For every Elliott or Dylan there have been, and continue to be, hundreds of pseudo-Guthries who have not made the big time. Rejecting their urban, middle-class backgrounds, they drift from campus to campus (or around a single campus), guitar in hand, passing themselves off as earthy, world-weary men of the soil. Early in the 1960s they were a subtle protest against the pseudo-intellectual sophistication of the academic community. They exuded a homey, nonconformist individuality and presumably were at peace with both nature and their own nature. Without a guitar, these "natural men" might easily be labeled beatniks. Armed with a guitar they were instantly transformed into "folkniks" or "folkies." By the 1970s the new stress on naturalism in dress, outlook, and bodily function would give the earlier hard-traveling life-style a new base of support, but now the guitar was incidental.

Guthrie is prized as painfully honest and frank, but there was always a part of him that was pure put-on. He passed himself off as a country bumpkin, in much the same way Will Rogers and Abraham Lincoln had. His prose was self-consciously filled with simple dialect. His songs, straightforward and simple to understand (at least on the immediate level), were performed with spartan simplicity. Yet Pete Seeger and others testified that although Guthrie ridiculed literary jargon and allusions, he was extremely well-read—ranging from medieval to modern literature.[27] Why then the consistent, tenacious "just folks" quality of his work? The answer is that Guthrie was a self-made myth. To identify with the masses, he had to remain one of the people. His power to influence, he believed, depended on his credibility. In part, his credibility depended on his continued folky ways. Yet, Guthrie was far from a Madison Avenue con man. He did not create one image as a mask while actually pursuing a contrary life-style. He consciously forced himself to adhere to his chosen image. Just as Abraham Lincoln retained his frontier mannerisms to maintain his political hold on the people, Guthrie retained his rural Oklahoma mannerisms to maintain his artistic hold on the people.[28]

There was yet another similarity between Guthrie and Lincoln. They both shared a militant faith in the average man's ability to shape society for the better. More precisely, Guthrie had the nineteenth-century American brand of optimism and affirmation. Woody was far closer to the mystic, confident individuality of Emerson than to the pragmatic social planners of his own era. It was after all Emerson who proclaimed, "I am defeated all the time; yet to victory I am born." It is no accident that Guthrie titled his autobiography *Bound For Glory,* and his collection of writings was titled *Born to Win.* Both Guthrie and Emerson attacked the political and economic establishment of their times. Both were sickened by American materialism and dismayed by America's moral blight. More importantly, both felt that man was born free with limitless powers. The difference between Guthrie and Emerson was also the crucial difference between Emerson and his contemporary, Andrew Jackson. Both Emerson and Jackson were for the people, but Jackson was of the people. Guthrie too, perhaps more than any artist of his time, had earned his common-man image. With all his faults and contradictions, he was clearly the quintessential proletarian man.

Few would deny that Woody Guthrie has been mythologized, but there is little agreement on what part of him is myth. Similarly, almost everybody agrees that Guthrie is relevant, but there is no consensus on how and why he is relevant. Some observers, like musical arranger Milton Okun, simply see Guthrie as a classic American songwriter. For Okun, "This Land Is Your Land" is "our national folk anthem" and "So Long, It's Been Good to Know You" is "a parting song on a par with 'Auld Lang Syne.'"[29] Some, like radical critic Irwin Silber, constantly stress that Guthrie was a true revolutionary whose current, indirect popularity "thru the voices of contemporary radiclib culture heroes represents not triumph but travesty," since his really radical writing has been obscured by a preoccupation with a few of his most popular songs.[30]

Several more balanced, less involved interpretatations of Guthrie have appeared over the years, but even these tend to center on narrow aspects of Guthrie's life that are of particular interest to his interpreters. John Greenway, in his path-breaking *American Folksongs of Protest* in 1953, saw Guthrie largely as a logical development of the rural hard-times school of folk-protest. Although Greenway is a general Guthrie admirer, he goes out of his way to note Guthrie's all too human faults, especially his infidelities to his wives and children. Guthrie supporters are often quite sensitive about any criticism of Woody by those they consider his moral inferiors. Gordon Friesen, editor of *Broadside,* scored Millard Lampell, a former member of the Almanac Singers, for describing Woody as a "bastard," "irresponsible," a drunkard "deserting those he cared for most," a man "looking for something he couldn't name." Friesen insisted that Guthrie "knew exactly what he was looking for" and "named it in almost everything he wrote."[31]

Later, in 1966, Greenway wrote an impassioned article that centered on what Woody's artistic genius represented and reflected. Here Greenway set forth the theory that Guthrie's radicalism and poetic creativity both could have stemmed from the genetic disease which had made him an invalid. Greenway believed that Guthrie's most creative period was between 1939 and 1948, and that while Woody had written some 1,400 songs during his life, the important thing was that from "fifty to a hundred" of the songs were as good as one could "find in all American folksong." Greenway could not imagine a "more harmless, more innocent captive of the cynical left" than Guthrie. Greenway's final judgment of Guthrie was that "he had genius as a poet-composer, mediocrity as a singer, and gullibility as a proletarian."[32] In 1971 R. Serge Denisoff, a sociologist, presented a detached, balanced interpretation of Guthrie's place in the political folksong movement. In his book, *Great Day Coming: Folk Music and the American Left,* Denisoff depicts Guthrie as a somewhat quixotic individual, torn between his own career ambitions and a feel for the proletarian struggle. As a communist, Guthrie was an outsider looking in, just as he was outside the mainstream of the entertainment world as a singer.[33]

Most popular accounts of Guthrie see him as a quaint rural drifter who loved America and loved people—especially poor people. That superficial assessment is not far off. However, the important thing is not only what Guthrie was really like, but what people thought he was like. It is Guthrie the legend rather than Guthrie the man that excites this generation of Americans. No amount of cool detailed scholarship can destroy a legend which is born anew every time a teenager listens to a Guthrie song or reads *Bound For Glory*. As Lillian Roxon noted, Woody was "the man you sang like in the early sixties."[34] For a smaller but important number of singers, the legendary Guthrie will remain, if not the man to sing like, at least the man to look and act like. His life-style has been passed on now for two generations, but it is far from shopworn. Indeed, its relevance seems to have grown throughout the past decade.

From our vantage point, Guthrie appears as a prophet. His life-style, songs, and writing clearly outlined the social battleground of the 1960s and 1970s. Who can doubt that the writer of "This Land Is Your Land" would be in the thick of the fight against pollution? Likewise, it is inconceivable that the Guthrie who condemned American intervention in Korea from its beginning would not have fought against American involvement in Vietnam even more vehemently. And would it not be fitting for the man who wrote "Pastures of Plenty," "Deportee," and other moving songs about the plight of migrant workers to be standing on the line with Cesar Chavez's striking farmworkers? Could the original devotee of hard traveling have resisted the freedom rides into the heart of Dixie? Could Woody, the enthusiastic exponent of the sit-down strike, have stood aloof from the sit-ins against segregation? While Guthrie's body was chained to a bed, his style pervaded the slogans and strategies of recent American radicals. Contemporary slogans like Power to the People, Right On, Shut It Down, and Make Love—Not War did not, of course, come from Guthrie's pen, but these chants seem to spring naturally from his lips.

Moreover, Guthrie's physical presence peers at us from

all corners of the youth culture. The wild long hair, the faded denims, the careless and outlandish combinations of clothes, and the profanity were all natural to Woody long before they became modish symbols for studied counter culturists. In short, Guthrie was an original alienated man and a natural enemy of bourgeois society. He was a living counter culture and perhaps the one American of the 1940s who could step into the Broadway cast of *Hair* and be perfectly at home. Simple, poetic, bawdy, militant, and erratic—Guthrie was singer Bob Dylan, political activist Jerry Rubin, and poet Allen Ginsberg rolled into one.

Nevertheless, Guthrie is a prophet without honor among the young. Contemporary youths know only a few of his most famous songs. The hip subculture is now overwhelmingly urban, while Guthrie was essentially a piece of rural Americana reacting to the Depression. The affluent now generation largely find Guthrie's songs corny, artless, and irrelevant. Yet the Guthrie legend continues to be passed on by a small, esoteric, but influential group of folksingers and folklorists. To them, Woody is an idol, not because he was a classic model, but because he was so obviously authentic. Guthrie has in one way or another influenced all of America's leading folksingers—Bob Dylan, Joan Baez, Phil Ochs, Pete Seeger, Judy Collins, and Tom Paxton, to name a few. With the exception of Seeger, they no longer carry on Guthrie's music or ideas, but they do carry on the Guthrie legend of the folk writer-performer as a social and cultural hero. They speak Woody's name with reverence and accept him unthinkingly, as children accept the Puritans and George Washington. At the same time, folk purists have embraced Guthrie as the one artist who did not prostitute his art for commercial gain. Testimonials to his genius and virtue continue to roll in from the pages of folk periodicals and scholarly journals and from the lips of folksingers. Only a few academicians have seriously considered Guthrie's weaknesses, and even they have been captivated by his influence and mystique.

Yet it is less important what Guthrie was like, and more

important what singers like Dylan, Baez, and Ochs think he was like. For these contemporary artists are the models for youth, and Guthrie now influences largely through his musical heirs. There are a few current performers who traveled with Woody and knew him well, Pete Seeger and Jack Elliott, for example. However, these sidekicks never became commercial successes and like Guthrie, they influence largely by their effect on the commercial stars of the folk field.

Guthrie had been on the road before Kerouac, howling before Ginsberg, and on the left when it was really dangerous to be there. Woody had been militantly antiestablishment before there was a popularly defined establishment. He undramatically pursued his unique life-style long before "doing your own thing" became *de rigueur* for commercial singers. Could he view contemporary America, Guthrie would inevitably recognize that he had, indeed, "been there and gone." Those who knew him personally and those who knew him only through his songs and imitators could sincerely say at his death in 1967, "So Long, It's Been Good to Know You."

5: Phil Ochs: A Minstrel's Search for Martyrdom

You're not a folksinger, you're a journalist [1]
—*Bob Dylan to Phil Ochs (1965)*

Dylan's heated slap at Phil Ochs was rather off target. Ochs had been a journalist as a college student, but from the moment he became a professional folksinger, he fancied himself an agitator. Like most topical writers, he drifted between the worlds of art and propaganda, never comfortable in either. The commercial pressures of the musical world made him suspect—a potential copout to fame or fortune. The bitter political fringe world of the SDS (Students for a Democratic Society) and Yippies (Youth International Party) turned him into narrow roads of thought and demanded an allegiance that cut him off from a wider youth-oriented audience. After 1968, Ochs increasingly moved toward despair, the Yippies, and the philosophy of the absurd (earlier adopted by Bob Dylan). Ochs's talent was as a biting, satirical missionary to guilt-ridden, affluent liberals and especially to their aimless children, but he yearned to be a hero of the left.

Thus, when his commercial success waned, it was easy to join the theatre of the absurd, easy to turn his back on a dwindling audience and a complacent society.

Like other comfortable middle-class children who turned to radicalism, Ochs was a product of the turbulent 1960s. If rebelling against your father is often necessary developmental task, as psychiatrist Bruno Bettelheim suggests, then Ochs finished his chore. Phil was born December 19, 1940, in El Paso, Texas. His father, a Jewish army physician, served at the local military base, and the family led a nomadic existence as Dr. Ochs was transferred to various veterans hospitals. Phil grew up in several places. Although he has spent most of his professional life in New York and California, he attended high school at Virginia's famous Staunton Military Academy with Senator Barry Goldwater's son Michael. Young Goldwater edited the school literary magazine and published Phil's first writing—a short story about a rabbit run down on the highway.[2]

Phil liked Staunton, where his main outside interests were weight-lifting and visiting the racetrack. According to Ochs, he "was involved in providing a hood exterior for [his] soft middle-class inner being." He enjoyed country music and played clarinet, saxophone, and drums in Staunton's marching band. He recalls being impressed by Senator Goldwater's military manner, when he spoke at Ochs's graduation. Phil also liked John Wayne war movies and admitted a tendency to "romanticize the military." Like Jerry Rubin, the Yippie spokesman and a personal friend, Ochs was almost an all-American boy. Ochs the military marching band member is the perfect counterpart to Rubin the Eagle Scout.[3]

Like Rubin and other youthful counter-culturists, Ochs was radicalized in college. After graduating from Staunton, Phil enrolled at Ohio State University, but soon dropped out temporarily to hobo around the country, Woody Guthrie-style. While jailed for vagrancy in Florida, he wrote his first song, "Three Dreams," with the help of a Negro prisoner. When he returned to Ohio State, he luckily was assigned to room with Jim Glover, a proficient folksinger. Glover would later have a minor success as one half of the musical Jim and Jean duo, and his influence pushed Phil solidly into the folk milieu. Ochs's life found a new focus. He became a journalism major, took up the guitar seriously, and moved toward campus activism. As a college junior, Phil joined Glover and other students in a folksinging group officially known as "The Sundowners'" but sometimes called "The Singing Socialists." The same year Ochs organized the *Word,* a new mimeo newspaper, and became managing editor of *Sundial,* the student humor magazine. He also wrote for the official student newspaper, but after his pro-Castro article brought protests from students and administrators, he was demoted to the post of music reviewer.

This direct censorship, which Ochs euphemistically labeled his "first taste of Free American Journalism" helped him decide to drop out of school. He went to Cleveland and found a job singing in a bar. There he met Bob Gibson, a talented veteran folksinger. Glover and Gibson were no doubt Phil's most important early musical influences. That same year, 1962, Ochs left to seek his fortune in New York.[4] In the 1930s the disenchanted Ochs might easily have become a young hobo; in the 1940s or 1950s he might have found his niche among resident campus bohemians in Columbus, Chicago, or New York. But Phil was a child of the 1960s, and his political activism and folk talent pushed him down the road of topical song. There were many "new frontiers" in 1962, and one of the least recognized was the revival of protest music, heralded that year by the appearance of *Broadside* magazine.

The Greenwich Village coffeehouse scene offered grim prospects to Ochs in 1962. Topical music was in its infancy. The big folk stars were clean-cut college trios who sang slickly arranged traditional music. Harder hitting singers like Jack Elliott and Dave Van Ronk made the rounds of folk "baskethouses," singing and passing the basket for nickels and dimes. Another newcomer, Bob Dylan, had joined the Village ranks a year before Ochs arrived. The folk crowd was split into two distinct camps. One younger group opted for new topical music; another group tried to preserve traditional music intact. Dylan would soon carry the day for the younger group, and Ochs followed his lead. Meanwhile, Pete Seeger continued to sing topical songs, and he acted as an older model for both Ochs and Dylan. The civil rights crusade furnished the most obvious song topics. Martin Luther King's Southern campaigns were in full swing and cried out for commemoration. The Village audiences that passionately favored the movement longed for songs of identification. Ochs was one of several neophyte writers who supplied the demand for topical songs of social conscience.

Bob Dylan gave the movement a solid start by publishing "Blowin' in the Wind" in *Broadside* in May 1962. The song drew almost universal and astonished acclaim from the Village folk pros. No doubt both Dylan and the song had a profound effect on Ochs as he wandered about the Village looking for a mission and a style. He had met Dylan in 1962, right after Bob had written "Don't Think Twice, It's All Right," and Phil was awestruck. Looking back, Ochs felt "it was a jolt, a real blow to the ego, to meet somebody that good." Ochs claimed that from 1962 to 1964 Dylan "mostly . . . liked" Phil's songs but that "sometimes he hated them."[5] In any case, as Ochs concentrated on topical songs during this period, Dylan was obviously both his idol and his competition. From 1962 to 1965, Dylan ran interference for Ochs. Both writers published their songs in *Broadside;* but beginning with his second album, *The Freewheelin' Bob Dylan,* in May 1963, and continuing with his third album, *The Times They Are A-Changin',* in January 1964, Dylan popularized topical songs as a new art form. These two albums contained "Masters of War," "Hard Rain's A-Gonna Fall," "Talking World War III Blues," "With God on Our Side," "Only a Pawn in Their Game," "The Lonesome Death of Hattie Carroll," and the epoch-making "The Times They Are A-Changin'."

However, no sooner was Dylan into protest music than he opted out. His next album, *Another Side of Bob Dylan,* in

August 1964, sang a bitter farewell to protest with such songs as "I Shall Be Free," "It Ain't Me Babe," and the explicitly antipolitical manifesto, "My Back Pages," Hereafter, Dylan's songs were personal cultural comments, wrapped in artistic prose code. The king of topical protest had left his throne shortly after gaining it.

Ochs stepped into the vacuum and became the acknowledged leader of topical song. In April 1964 Elektra Records released his first album with the blatantly topical title, *All the News That's Fit to Sing*. Most of the album songs had already been published in *Broadside*, but now the wider audience that Dylan had created was ready for them. Such songs as "Thresher," "Too Many Martyrs," "Ballad of William Worthy," "Talking Cuban Crisis" and "Talking Vietnam" did indeed suggest that the album was a musical newspaper. Ochs's next two albums, *I Ain't Marching Anymore* (1965) and *Phil Ochs in Concert* (1966), solidified his claim to Dylan's former kingdom. The Vietnam war was escalating, the Watts riots had erupted, and Ochs's music traced a steady leftward path, marching in unison with the rise of a militant, campus centered "New Left." His first album had mirrored the sentiments of the Democratic Party's left wing, with its cautious diplomatic desire to accept communist nations as valid governments and its fervent support of civil rights in the South. However, Phil's 1965 album put him clearly beyond the establishment left. Such songs as "Here's to the State of Mississippi" and "Talking Birmingham Jam" showed the typical commitment to the Southern Negro, but "I Ain't Marching Anymore" and "Draft Dodger Rag" were frankly pacifist ballads. "In the Heat of the Summer" focused on the plight of rioting blacks in Northern ghettoes and "Links on the Chain" asked organized labor to remember when the police were "bustin' the heads of many a union man." "Links on the Chain" was a clever polemic, arguing that the civil rights demonstrators were only doing what the older union members had taught them—"that you gotta fight, you gotta strike, to get what you are owed." The song ended by telling the unions that "it's only fair to ask . . .

which side are you on?" The entire *I Ain't Marching Anymore* album had an ultimatum mood about it.

There were ultimatums to the white South, the Northern
cities, organized labor, and the armed services. Ochs summed
them up in the title song when he told the listener to "call it
peace or treason, call it love or call it reason," but he wasn't
"marching anymore." On the liner notes, Phil described the
title song as bordering between "pacifism and treason,
combining the best qualities of both." Commenting on
"Draft Dodger Rag," he compared the Viet Cong soldier who
screamed his hatred of Americans while being shot by a firing
squad to his American counterpart who stayed "up nights
thinking of ways to" escape the army. The album's one
contradiction was "That Was the President," a warm memorial ballad to John Kennedy. Phil explained that his Marxist
friends could not understand why he wrote it, and that was
probably one reason that he was not a Marxist. However,
Ochs backed away from the hero worship of this ballad by
explaining that "after the assassination Fidel Castro aptly
pointed out that only fools could rejoice at such a tragedy, for
systems, not men, are the enemy."[6] Overall, the album established Phil's radical credentials.

With his 1966 album, Ochs moved more clearly into the
camp of the New Left. The *Phil Ochs in Concert* record was
taped live at New York and Boston appearances in the winter
of 1965-1966 and included several politically barbed song
introductions. Before singing one song, Phil defined a liberal
as someone who was "ten points to the left of center in good
times," but "ten points to the right of center" when anything
"affected him personally." The liner notes symbolized the
album's mood with eight sensitive poems by Chinese Communist leader Mao Tse-tung, capped by the question, "Is
This the Enemy?" Mao appeared again in the opening song,
"I'm Going to Say It Now," a ballad written for the Berkeley
Free Speech Movement. In this song the singer tells college
officials that whereas they are supporting Chiang Kai-shek,
he is "supporting Mao," and that when he has "something to
say, sir," he is "going to say it now." Another song, "Cops of
the World," reflected the new "policeman-as-pig" campaign

coming out of the San Francisco Bay area. The album also included "Ringing of Revolution," a tongue-in-cheek call for insurrection; "Bracero," a plea for the Mexican farm-worker, and "Cannons of Christianity," a swipe at the hypocrisy of organized religion. However, the key album song was "Love Me, I'm a Liberal." This ballad commemo-rated Ochs' break with the patient, Democratic left. All eight verses mocked the establishment liberal who was afraid to move ideologically and invariably declined to put his body where his mouth was. Ochs ridiculed people who attended "civil rights rallies" and knocked "the old D.A.R." (Daugh-ters of the American Revolution), and who loved "Puerto Ricans and Negroes," until they moved next door, who put down Southerners but refused to bus their own children, who read *New Republic* and had "memorized Lerner and Golden" until they almost felt like "a Jew," yet when it came "to times like Korea," were still "Red, White, and Blue." Each verse ended with the sarcastic refrain, "Love Me, I'm a Liberal."[7] The 1966 album was a further response to the escalating Vietnam war, a declaration that Ochs was moving out of the system and taking his stand with the beleaguered young troops of the SDS.

From the start Ochs was anxious to talk about his art. Unlike Dylan, he gave a steady round of interviews on topical music. He demonstrated a need to rationalize his work—to show why he was on the stage instead of in the streets. The 1965 album's liner pointedly noted that Phil had been doing it as well as singing it. Ochs related that he had been with striking miners in Hazard, Kentucky. He remembered sing-ing on "the tops of speaker-trucks . . . in cold weather at countless rallies." He wondered if he would be investigated by Congress and waited for a "faceless American Legion-naire" to grab him by the collar. No doubt he looked forward to possible persecution with a martyr's resignation, since he added:

> I realize that I can't feel any nobility for what I write because I know my life could never be as moral as my songs. I know I'm sticking my neck out and I know I'll be attacked.[8]

As early as March 1963, Ochs published a short essay in *Broadside* on "The Need for Topical Music," filled with optimistic visions about the future of protest songs. Phil explained that "one good song with a message" could make its point "more deeply to more people than a thousand rallies." He lamented that only two causes—civil rights and the peace movement—seemed able to rouse people from their apathy, since he felt every "newspaper headline" was "a potential song."[9] Not surprisingly, from his first song in *Broadside*'s fourteenth issue in October 1962, Phil excelled in the news-type ballad. During *Broadside*'s first twenty-five issues, Ochs was the most frequent contributor, publishing seventeen songs. The other three *Broadside* stars during this period were Malvina Reynolds with sixteen songs, Bob Dylan with thirteen, and Pete Seeger with twelve. Phil was so deep into the *Broadside* movement that in 1963 he was selling the magazine between sets of his road performances.[10]

However, Ochs was hardly a slave to *Broadside*'s frankly political approach to music, even while he wrote within its tradition. In 1965 at a symposium on topical songs, he indicated support for two revolutions in music—the one a "revolution in songwriting, adding perceptive protest and valid poetry," the other a revolution of music, carrying on the rock-and-roll, rhythm-and-blues tradition of the 1950s. Both revolutions were important, he argued, because they communicated reality with "beauty, soul, and entertainment." Phil felt he now had to work on the "art" of his songs "rather than the politics." He would now "rather listen to a good song" promoting segregation, than "a bad song" for "integration." He claimed he did not want to be a "spokesman for the Left, for SNCC . . . or for anybody," except himself. Instead he wanted "to be destroyed by art," to hear songs so poetic and musically exciting that they could turn him "inside out with the communication of feeling."[11]

Undoubtedly Ochs was influenced by Bob Dylan's recent move toward personal rather than topical songs. Indeed, Ochs quickly defended Dylan against charges that he had sold out. In an open letter to Irwin Silber (editor of *Sing*

Out!, who had roundly criticized Dylan) and to writer Paul
Wolfe (who had awarded Dylan's "topical crown" to Ochs),
Phil ridiculed their political approach. He facetiously suggested that Silber award an annual prize to "the most
militant protestor in the form of a Silber bullet," and that
Dylan should be made to stand in the corner and write
" 'Forgive Me, Joe Hill' at least a thousand times." Ochs
considered Dylan's newer, personal songs "as brilliant as
ever," and indicated he was following Bob's lead and writing
only "out of an urge to write, period." Phil concluded by
adopting a mock critical rage:

> Who does Dylan think he is, anyway? When I grow used to an
> artist's style I damn well expect him not to disappoint me by
> switching it radically. My time is too precious to waste trying
> to change a pattern of my thought. If you're reading this, Bob,
> you might as well consider this an open letter to you too.
> Where do you get off writing about your own experiences?
> Don't you realize there's a real world out there, a world of
> bombs and elections, folk music critics and unemployed
> folksingers.[12]

Throughout 1965 Ochs praised Dylan's new attitudes
and songs.[13] It marked the high tide of his Dylan worship. Yet
Dylan had recently flatly rejected Ochs's work. Phil felt that
Bob thought his work was "political and therefore bullshit."
As Ochs put it, "Here's the man I most respect in the world
. . . telling me that—'hey, your writing is bullshit.'"[14]
Anthony Scaduto's biography of Dylan quotes Bob telling
Ochs:

> The stuff you're writing is bullshit, because politics is bull-
> shit. It's all unreal. The only thing that's real is inside you.
> Your feelings. Just look at the world you're writing about and
> you'll see you're wasting your time. The world is, well . . . it's
> just absurd.[15]

Ochs's ego carried him through this crisis. He concluded
that he was into one thing and Dylan into another. Phil
considered his art a form of "social realism," and he criticized
Dylan for rejecting any art form. Whereas Ochs felt Dylan
gave in to the world's absurdity, he (Ochs) was disturbed

enough by the absurd to write about it and deal with it. Thus, though you could not "defeat the absurdity of the world," you had to make the attempt. For Ochs that was "morality . . . religion . . . art . . . life."[16]

Pro or con, other critics too usually saw Phil in terms of the changing Bob Dylan. Paul Wolfe saw Ochs as the new leader of topical song. Wolfe described Phil's 1965 *I Ain't Marching Anymore* album as unique in its "clarity . . . contrasting shades of humor and bitterness, subtlety, irony, and power." Moreover, its "singularity of focus" made it "the most important record" to emerge from the topical song movement.[17] In the same year Don West, founder of the Highlander Folk School, concluded that although Ochs made "some good propaganda now and then," he was not "a good musician." At best his songs expressed "some good sentiments, frequently in poor verse."[18] West, a poet by trade, simply wrote off Ochs as unpoetic. Music critic Nat Hentoff seemed to agree. He felt most of Ochs's lyrics—"a few ballads excepted"—were "flatly, prosaically polemical," as well as "one-dimensional and drearily dated in style."[19] It all boiled down to whether you judged Phil's songs on an artistic basis or a political one. Few critics were able to measure his songs on balance. Phil himself had recently adopted the artistic standards his work failed to meet. Yet Ochs took the artistic criticism with forced humor, apparently deciding that it was better to be wanted for murder than not to be wanted at all. For example, his 1968 book of essays and songs, *The War Is Over,* included a page of short critical comments on his work, titled "The Critics Raved." Among the entries were:

> *High Fidelity:* "His melodies are about as inventive as the average Tibetan chant."
> *Little Sandy Review:* "Fifteenth-rate topical songs by a tenth-rate journalist."
> *Esquire:* "Too bad his guitar playing would not suffer much were his right hand webbed."[20]

Phil's next album, *Pleasures of the Harbor* in 1967, attempted to raise his artistic level.[21] The effort had mixed results. It included Ochs's first long songs, "Pleasures of the Harbor" (a meandering abstract of personal consciousness) and "The Crucifixion" (a powerful parable which linked a never-identified Jesus with contemporary radicals and martyrs). "Crucifixion" was poetic, but its strength was in the sharp, biting political parallels. It was probably the high point of Ochs's artistic endeavors. The remaining songs were subtler than earlier efforts, but the prose was usually forced and heavy. The one frankly topical song, "Outside of a Small Circle of Friends," a satiric view of mass passivity, was easily the strongest song besides "Crucifixion." Questions of artistic merit aside, the album did not sell as well as Ochs's earlier efforts. Phil's move toward longer poetic songs followed the footsteps of Bob Dylan; but Dylan had been there and gone, and the young audience had gone with him.[22]

Dylan had long since moved into the rock scene and Ochs's refusal to follow partly accounted for his declining popularity. But Phil was as much a victim of politics as of musical trends. As the Vietnam war had intensified from 1965 to 1967, Ochs's natural constituency, the young college left, had grown impatient with mere protest songs. The path of the Students for a Democratic Society (SDS) mirrored the change. Once Ochs was their darling, but now they were past singing or concerts and were on the march. Phil tried to bridge the gap. He became more cynical in his view, more militant in his verse, but he never caught up with the new movement because topical songs were no longer a viable vehicle of leadership. What you did was now much more important than what you said or how you said it. After 1968 Ochs would become a more active foot soldier in the antiwar movement. But meanwhile his political frustration became increasingly apparent during 1967 and 1968.

In a 1966 interview Ochs still appeared more independent than ideological. He had praise for the Viet Cong "as the last workable bulwark against Communist China," and he gave measured support to Castro. However, he acknowledged that he would be shot for singing in China. Phil wanted to be a "militant critic" in a wealthy society. In regard to labels he explained:

> I can't belong to any groups because all groups are essentially self-defeating to an artist. I can't accept the Left Wing although I am part of it.[23]

Increasingly, Phil would find it easier to join groups and seek labels.

By late 1967 Ochs was already sounding the street theatre "war is over" theme that would pervade his songs after 1968. In a *Village Voice* article he proclaimed that Lyndon Johnson was "more absurd than wrong." Ochs now felt that "the spiritually depraved American public" could not accept "blunt truth served on a negative platter." What was needed were "joyful, energized, magnificently absurd demonstrations fitted to the demands of an electronic, cinematic era. For if the government did not "have the courage of their reality to declare" the war was on, the people should at least have enough courage of "imagination to declare it over." Ochs had crossed the border and become a Yippie camp follower. His optimism was gone. He now saw the Vietnam war as "an amphetamine trip," which reflected "the spiritual disease" that had distorted every American principle.[24] In a period of absurdity and insanity, was it not more effective to speak absurdly and act madly? Ochs's answer was affirmative.

Phil had to revise his philosophy of protest music to fit the times, and his new "Summa Theologica" was displayed in a long, three-installment interview for *Broadside*, early in 1968. He recalled that in 1965 he had predicted that songwriting's increased literacy would raise popular music's standards. Now, however, he saw 1965 as the aesthetic pinnacle, followed by a period of general decline. Phil saw a direct correlation between the path of music and that of America. According to Ochs, artists like Dylan, Donovan, and Tim Hardin had reached their peak soon after their first heady acquaintance with rock music. Shortly thereafter, the new folk-rock music was honed to a commercial formula and started its downward path. For Ochs, the music of 1968, when compared to that of 1965, was superficial, "more physical and less mental."[25] Musical criticism had also declined. Phil argued that critics like Bob Shelton of the *New York Times*, who had followed the protest-song movement from its start, had become "mere chroniclers." The critics had stopped looking at the music and focused instead on new, interesting performers. In the process, critics became performers themselves at best, and at worst they functioned as cult builders, substituting "adjectives for logic."[26]

The "cult-builders" had obviously not been building up Ochs, and Phil indirectly blamed his obscurity on music's commercialization. It was not that political music had been neglected, but that honest music had declined. Ochs felt that "political songs" were a misnomer, since any artful song irrespective of subject could reflect political realities. For example, he thought that Dylan's earliest folk-rock songs described America's "spiritual crisis," even before an accelerated Vietnam war made that crisis apparent. By 1968, however, Ochs felt his earlier, consistent praise of Dylan had been an unhealthy "form of hero worship," which Phil had finally recovered from. For Dylan too had declined from the heights of 1965. In his recent albums he was overextended and like "the emperor without his clothes," with the critics too blinded by Dylan's legend to criticize his work. Ochs also charged that the older, folk-oriented recording companies, notably Vanguard and Elektra, had joined the commercial thrust and had begun "grasping for riches." Phil criticized his former company, Elektra, for gaudily advertising new groups like The Doors.[27] In *Broadside*'s next issue Jac Holzman, head of Elektra, replied by charging Ochs with hypocrisy. Holzman stated that no other Elektra artist had "checked sales figures more carefully or more frequently than Phil." He did not condemn Ochs, since "awareness of public acceptance" was desirable, he simply charged Phil with envy.[28]

There was a "sour-grapes" ring to many of Ochs's comments after 1968. Doubtless he felt betrayed as popular music moved away from serious message songs. While the country was being torn by a tragic war, music steadily moved away from reality and toward individual mystique. In 1968, the year that Eugene McCarthy challenged Lyndon Johnson for the Presidency, Ochs clearly concluded that the way back to the musical audience was through the political audience. He lent his name and services to McCarthy's campaign almost from the start. In May, at a McCarthy fund-raising rally in Madison Square Garden, the *New York Times* reported that the greatest applause went to the "shaggy" Ochs "for his antiwar song, 'I Ain't Marching Anymore.'"[29] When it became clear that McCarthy was not going to be nominated, Phil joined the demonstrators in the Chicago streets. The *Village Voice* reported that during a Yippie-organized rally in Grant Park, Ochs had transformed the gathering "into some sort of prayer session," by again singing the boisterous ballad, "I Ain't Marching Anymore."[30] Surrounded by leftist leaders Jerry Rubin, Dave Dellinger, and Tom Hayden, Ochs had finally caught up with his old political audience in the madness of Mayor Daley's Chicago. McCarthy had tried the system and Ochs with him. Both concluded that the political process no longer worked.

Ochs's new, more militant mood showed clearly in his next album, *Tape from California,* released in September, 1968. Like his last record, it included some long, abstract, personal ballads like the title song, but the best cuts were the two topical Vietnam protests, "White Boots Marching in a Yellow Land" and "The War Is Over." The latter song was particularly bitter. Here Ochs clearly renounced his role as social critic. He would not be just another angry artist "painting angry signs," using his insight "just to blind the blind." To do so was to play "a grisly game," in which one person was guilty while the other got "to point the blame."[31] Phil had now divorced himself from the war and moved into an existentialist world. However, the album also contained Ochs's "Joe Hill," a long, often historically inaccurate, spirited song biography of the Wobbly hero. Hill, hardly an existentialist dropout, seemed out of place here, but perhaps he too was part of Ochs's escape from the present.

Joan Baez, 1967, sings on the Washington Monument grounds after the Daughters of the American Revolution refused her the use of Constitution Hall. Secretary of the Interior Stewart Udall granted Joan the use of the monument grounds.

Joan with husband Paul Harris in 1970.

Phil Ochs (third from the left) with Brian Flanigan, Jerry Rubin, and Stewe Albert during a press conference in Paris in 1970, when Rubin announced that their organization, the "Yippies," would confederate with Timothy Leary and the Black Panthers.

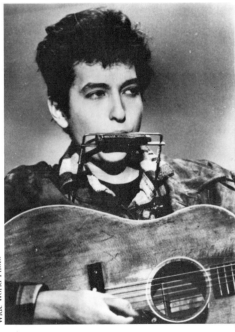

Above, Bob Dylan as he appeared in 1963, and right, in concert at Madison Square Garden in 1974.

The 1968 album was Phil's second for A & M Records (after leaving Elektra in 1967), but his first record with orchestral accompaniment. Yet Ochs did not move from acoustical to electric guitar until 1969. Indeed, back in 1966 he had delighted in ridiculing electronic rock groups who mistook "shouting for singing." Phil argued that electric music must be balanced by control and that most groups who intended "to become masters of volume" had ended up "prisoners of noise."[32] By 1969 Ochs too had imprisoned his lyrics with electronic sound. His next album, *Rehearsals for Retirement*,[33] was in typical folk-rock style, complete with electric sidemen and sound-on-sound arrangements. This record explicitly announced Phil's withdrawal from institutional America. The cover showed a tombstone which read:

Phil Ochs
(American)
Born: El Paso, Texas 1940
Died: Chicago, Illinois 1968

On the back cover was a poem describing America's decay. Roughly half the songs detailed the same topic. One ballad, "Pretty Smart on My Part," satirized an irrational, middle-American fear of the radical young. Another song, "I Kill Therefore I Am," depicted policemen as sadistic status seekers. Still another cut pictured the Chicago demonstrators of 1968 as an early Woodstock nation, trampled by American paranoia. Only one song, "Another Age," had hope for the future. Though the verses described American decline, the chorus asked us to "pray for the aged" since it was "the dawn of another age." The remaining songs commented on Ochs's withdrawal from American society and his musical retirement. The title song and "Doesn't Lenny Live Here Anymore" suggested that America had become too corrupt an environment to support honest artists. However, Phil's personal dropout manifesto appeared in the ballad, "My Life," which told more about Ochs's self-image than anything he has written. In it he recalled his once joyful life when he wrote "like a God" and all his "melodies were sweet." Although everyone begged him "to buy," he slipped through their "scheme." He felt "lucky to fail," since it showed his "life was not" up "for sale." And so he now faced "the land" where he was "so out of place," only to cast a "curse" and gain the "grace" of knowing where he stood. In closing the song, Phil tells America to "take everything" he owns, but to leave his "life alone." All in all this album provided an artful, if uneven, goodbye.

Unfortunately, Ochs could not resist giving an encore adieu and amen. Late in 1970 he released his last album, *Phil Ochs' Greatest Hits*.[34] The record was largely a put-on. The front cover showed Phil dressed up in early Elvis Presley style, in a gold-spangled suit, sporting an electric guitar. On the back cover each album song was inscribed on its own gold record. Above, large print proclaimed: "50 Phil Ochs Fans Can't Be Wrong!" It was an ironic twist to Ochs's declining popularity, but the songs themselves failed to amuse. The main album themes were extensions of the last two albums— America's decline and Ochs's rejection of the nation. The songs "Jim Dean of Indiana" and especially "Boy in Ohio" suggested that Ochs, like James Dean, was an innocent soul drifting through a corrupt society. Such ballads as "One Way Ticket Home," "Chords of Fame," and "No More Songs" reiterated Phil's retirement and idealistic rejection of America. Now, however, the songs were hasty and poorly drawn. The fancier musical mixing only drowned out some lyrics. On the first side Phil sang that although he would "be in exile now," it did not matter since "everyplace was the same." In that mood, every record he made would be the same. Ochs should have said his final farewell with the more artful *Rehearsals for Retirement*.

In the years since his last recording venture, Phil has continued to dog the footsteps of the rapidly aging "New Left." In October 1971 Ochs and David Ifshin, a former president of the National Students Association, were detained in both Uruguay and Argentina after meeting with student leaders during their Latin American tour.[35] Earlier that year Phil and Yippie leader Jerry Rubin had visited Charlie Manson, the mystic cult murderer, in the Los

Angeles jail. Rubin reported that after they had "exchanged clenched fists," the three had a long rap session and that both Ochs and he "were visibly moved" by Manson's "strength and personal magnetism."[36] Ochs had not written any new songs since 1970 and had appeared infrequently in concert. However, at a New York concert in October 1972, Phil appeared on the bill with David Bromberg and Doc Watson. Ochs sang some of his old favorites, changed the words of "Here's to the State of Mississippi," to "Here's to the Government of Richard Nixon," and noted that he had been traveling around the world and working for peace in Indo-China. The emcee commented that Ochs had stopped writing during the past two years because he now questioned "a song's contribution to creating revolution." When asked what he was doing currently, Phil asked the audience what they were "doing now, tomorrow and next week while the war goes on."[37] Clearly Och's music was now totally divorced from his political activities. In late 1972 he broke his recording moratorium and put out a single record, "Kansas City Bomber," obviously inspired by the motion picture of the same name, starring Raquel Welch. The lyrics were printed in *Broadside* without comment or music. No doubt the editors were trying to be kind to an old hero.[38]

Ochs's career was an artistic tragedy. More importantly, it illustrated most of the difficulties and contradictions inherent in any merger of music and politics. Ochs was the most politicized professional singer of his era. Whereas older protest singers like Woody Guthrie had been shaped primarily by their social and economic backgrounds, Phil was a product of the 1960s as a whole. He was not a journalist as Bob Dylan quipped; more accurately Ochs was shaped by contemporary journalism. Phil's tragedy was generational as well as artistic. The sixties built some people up and broke others down. To Joan Baez the decade furnished new goals and new confidence; for Ochs the quickly shifting political terrain provided increasing chaos and growing artistic isolation.

Ochs was caught in a classic dilemma. He wanted to do

more than just sing. Increasingly he yearned to be a really radical activist. Yet the only way he could be a meaningful political force was to write and sing protest songs. Also, by 1965 he clearly felt that topical songs should emulate or even surpass the lyrical quality of the best contemporary popular music. This put Phil in a double bind. Not only was the audience for blatant protest songs fading, but after 1965 Ochs could not match the lyrical quality of the younger folk-rock artists following Dylan's footsteps. It was one thing to play second to Dylan as a topical writer. It was quite another to be just one more mediocre folksinger. To remain a straightforward political lyricist was to lose both the new mass audience and the increasingly militant and action-oriented New Left. To compose strictly lyrical songs while trying to be a street agitator was to pursue two unrelated activities, neither of which Ochs did well. Nevertheless, Phil chose the latter course. As a result, while his few topical songs remained high in quality, his artistic writing was usually mediocre, and his half-hearted political organizing activity hardly made him a hero of the steadily more explosive left.

By 1968 Ochs realized that he could not compete musically with the Beatles, or Dylan, or a score of others, and he turned to frank message music, wrapped in more modern arrangements. As his lyrics turned more militant, he gained some acceptance from the left, while his general audience grew smaller. Ochs was a minstrel; he needed the cheers and encouragement of the crowd. His creativity dried up at the same rate his concert audiences diminished. Phil's new, limited audience wanted a jester to mock society. No doubt the twin frustrations of his declining musical career and the faltering antiwar movement led Ochs to indulge the pessimism and cynicism always beneath the surface of his songs, but very evident in his prose writing and concert patter.

From his theme song, "I Ain't Marching Anymore," in 1965 to his virtual retirement from music in 1970, Ochs had been marching down an inevitable path. Each new year and musical trend encouraged the commercial rejection of Ochs's music. Meanwhile, each of Phil's songs came closer to a flat rejection of America and a personal identification with the martyred remnants of the New Left. Ochs never became a physical martyr, and his appearance as a defense witness for the Chicago Seven during their conspiracy trial illustrated his camp-follower connection to the youthful left. Phil's work for McGovern during 1972 illustrated his ambivalence toward the system. In 1972, as throughout the decade, he wandered between the liberal and radical camps without finding a resting place in either.

If Ochs's search for political martyrdom was inconclusive, his journey toward musical martyrdom was a technical triumph. There was a "bound for glory" theme that ran through his lyrics, yet Phil increasingly realized that he had had his glory and was bound for obscurity. It was not that his newer, more militant songs were too controversial; militant songs by nature became irrelevant. Yet Ochs wisely beat American culture to the punch. He rejected America politically before America could reject him culturally. He retired like the classic romantic hero—a man too pure for the corrupt world around him. Yet there was an air of serenity and inevitability around his musical departure. To fight the good fight and fail was hardly a disgrace. The victory had been in the struggle. As Christopher Lasch has noted in one of his more pessimistic moods, "American leftists have to fail. They have a particular flair for it."[39] It was now possible to see Ochs as an artistic martyr to inevitable, pernicious forces. His own earlier ballad, "Crucifixion" (probably his best work), might have been his own artistic epitaph. In ten long verses "Crucifixion" chronicles a martyr's life. The song is usually seen as a comment on the life and death of both Jesus and John Kennedy. Indeed, the most consistent theme running through Ochs's songs is that of the romantic martyr. It was no accident that Phil's first album contained the ballad, "Too Many Martyrs," about Medgar Evers, plus songs about William Worthy, a martyred mailman, and Lou Marsh, a murdered youth worker. Later Phil memorialized John Kennedy, Joe Hill, and James Dean in separate songs, while his musical version of Alfred Noyes's poem, "The

Highwayman," celebrated Bess, the landlord's daughter, as his lone feminine martyr.

Considering Ochs's preoccupation with martyrdom, the lyrics of "Crucifixion" could have more personal meaning. They may constitute Ochs's view of himself as a martyred musical agitator. The song described a man "chosen for a challenge" that was "hopelessly hard," a man who stood "on the sea" and shouted "to the shore." However, "ignorance" was "everywhere" and people had "their way"; while "success" was "an enemy to the losers of the day." The song asks who could want to harm "such a hero of the game," but the singer replies that he had "predicted it." The rebel's eyes had "been branded by the blind"; his threat had "been refined." The ballad concludes that the child had been created to be led to the slaughterhouse, and thus "the cycle of sacrifice" unwound. From first to last Phil Ochs had been a minstrel in search of martyrdom. If he mistook obscurity for martyrdom, perhaps that reflected the conspiratorial paranoia of that era. Yet Ochs was peculiarly talented. If he lacked the lyrical ability of a Bob Dylan, Randy Newman, or Don McLean, he remained the most talented political songwriter of the decade. If Ochs had not tried to change musically with the times, he could have continued to perfect his peculiar art form for smaller specialized audiences. As Thoreau wisely noted, an acorn cannot choose to be a peach tree if the environment is not favorable to oak trees.

6: Joan Baez: A Pacifist St. Joan

The 1960s were particularly hard on American heroes. Even John Kennedy, a legendary martyr in 1963, had his memory badly tarnished by the ugly results of his foreign policy. Thus it is noteworthy that Joan Baez's intellectual image soared during a period of general cynicism. Her rise in esteem was mostly a matter of timing, for Joan grew up with the decade. In 1960, during the earliest days of Camelot, she was a largely unknown nineteen-year-old singer with a gifted voice and a penchant for Anglo-American folk ballads. As events grew darker in 1963 and after, she gradually became an activist, both in the area of civil rights and universal nonviolence. In 1964 she demonstrated her concern symbolically by refusing to pay that portion of her income tax (60%) designated for defense spending.[1] The following year she funded an Institute for the Study of Nonviolence, headquartered in her hometown—Carmel, California.[2]

Baez's early diatribes against the nation-state were usually vague, but the accelerating Vietnam war documented most of her points. Joan was frankly and consistently radical in an age of polarization, and pacifist in an era of increasing violence. More importantly, she addressed herself to the problems of universal man, at a time when many American youths were vomiting on nationalism. Above all, there was her singing, which compensated for her early intellectual shallowness and general inarticulateness. Throughout the 1960s her crystal-clear voice soared through the soprano register, high above the political and social struggles. Always the most artful, distinct singer in the folk field, Joan shifted her repertory from the ancient balladry to protest songs, to Bob Dylan's prose songs, to country-and-western, and finally to her own compositions. Baez's record albums always sold well, but were never best sellers; and this relative lack of commercial popularity protected her political credibility. As the child of a decade of agitation, her attitudes and life-style evolved so smoothly that she seemed not to have changed at all. Joan blended into the protest tradition, into pacifism, into activism, into a publicized marriage and motherhood, into a vicarious martyrdom (as her husband, David Harris, went to jail for draft resistance), and finally into a national symbol for nonviolence.

Baez was an unlikely cultural heroine. Born in Staten Island, New York, in 1941, she was one of three sisters. Her father, a Mexican-born physicist, and her mother, of Scotch-English ancestry, met at Drew University in Madison, New Jersey, and the family moved around the country while Dr. Baez pursued his career as a researcher and consultant. The family's strong religious background may partly explain Joan's moral fervor. Her maternal grandfather was an Episcopal minister, while her paternal grandfather was a Catholic turned Methodist clergyman. Moreover, her parents were converts to the Quaker faith, though Joan remains religiously nonaligned. After attending high school in Palo Alto, California, she moved to Boston with her family in 1959 and became a college dropout after a month at Boston

University. By this time her largely untrained voice was already striking enough to make her a local star at Boston coffeehouses. The folk boom was just beginning (especially around the Eastern colleges) and Baez picked up songs and guitar technique from a number of semiprofessional folk-singers. That summer, Joan was a surprise sensation at the Newport Folk Festival, and she soon signed a recording contract with Vanguard Records—a small company which retained her loyalty for twelve years. Baez's initial record was released in 1960, followed by the first of many successful college-oriented concert tours, and Joan Baez was suddenly America's premier folksinger. She was all of twenty years of age.[3]

Like Bob Dylan, another famous folk dropout, Joan rejected a college education. In 1967, she asserted that college was just another way for parents "to hang on to their children." She could see putting up with the "trivia of college" to get professional training, but not because "your parents or society says you should."[4] Joan felt she "rebelled so completely" against education because her father's academic standing obligated her to be a "student-type." Dr. Baez had often disapproved of her ideas on "nonviolence and antinationalism"; and she noted with obvious satisfaction that though he "was peace-marching long before" his daughter, her radical swing left him "looking and acting . . . fairly moderate."[5] Moving to her father's left in regard to education and pacifism might have been part of a personal rebellion. In any case, Joan received a unique social education. American society was teaching a variety of lessons and she learned fast. Baez was immediately attracted to the civil rights crusade, probably because of her own childhood exposure to racism. Joan grew up in Redlands, California, in a cultural limbo. Her father had professional status, but she was not accepted by whites because she was dark and part Mexican, while the Mexican population disowned her because she could not speak Spanish. Later, when the family moved to Clarence Center, New York, a town of 800 people, Joan felt that "as far as they knew we were niggers."[6]

Baez was one of many folksingers who actively supported civil rights. When she attended the rally that climaxed the "March on Washington" in August 1963, Bob Dylan, Peter, Paul and Mary, and others performed with her. Yet, none of these had risked personal harm as Joan had, when she escorted a little black girl to her integrated school through a hostile crowd in Birmingham, Alabama, earlier that year. Nor did protest singers tend to involve themselves physically in such activities as the Student Free Speech Movement and the early protests against the Vietnam war. Joan was often a physical activist. In December 1964, at the University of California's Berkeley campus, Baez helped draw a large crowd to a rally protesting the banning of certain campus political activities and then marched into the University's administration building at the head of one thousand undergraduates who occupied the building for fifteen hours.[7]

On June 8, 1965, Joan sang at the SANE Emergency Rally on Vietnam, in Madison Square Garden, but before performing she told the crowd:

> This is mainly to the young people here, but really to everybody. . . . You must listen to your heart and do what it dictates. . . . If you feel that to . . . go to war is wrong, you have to say no to the draft. And if you young ladies think it is wrong to kill . . . you can say yes to the young men who say no to the draft.[8]

In August 1965, Joan joined a thousand anti-Vietnam demonstrators in picketing the White House. She later commented: "I don't think the President gives a damn."[9] Although it would be almost three years before she met her husband, David Harris, marriage to a draft resister seemed almost inevitable. For example, in 1966 there appeared a poster which pictured the three Baez sisters sitting on a bench, staring straight ahead, with the caption: "Girls Say Yes to Boys Who Say No."

After continuing her antiwar and civil rights activities in 1966, Baez made her first concert tour abroad when she visited Japan in January 1967. At her Tokyo concert, which was later shown on Japanese television, the Japanese translator admitted that he left out all of Baez's political remarks at the urging of a man who identified himself as a CIA agent. Thus, when Joan explained the song, "What Have They Done to the Rain" (about atomic fallout), the translator stated only that "the show was being televised." When she interpreted her subtle antiwar song, "Saigon Bride," he said only, "This is a song about the Vietnam war." And when Joan told the audience she had refused to pay her taxes as a protest against the Vietnam war, the translator said only, "Taxes are high in the United States." On balance, Joan's trip was not a political success. She said she came to Japan "first as a human being, second as a pacifist, and third as a folksinger." However, the Japanese tended to accept her primarily as a folksinger, only secondarily as a human being, and hardly at all as a pacifist.[10]

Back in the United States, Joan became more vigorous. She was arrested in Oakland, California, in October 1967 for blocking the Armed Forces Induction Center and served a ten-day prison sentence. Two months later she served thirty days for the same offense. Her mother, then fifty-four years old, accompanied her both times. As Joan put it, "My Mother's been to jail with me twice now. We did civil disobedience together."[11] During her October sit-in, Joan met David Harris for the first time. In a rather unique courtship, Harris visited Joan during her second jail term, and they agreed to tour selected colleges and cities to speak for draft resistance. Joan would usually give a concert, and then David and she would speak about the resistance. In the middle of their tour, in March 1968, they were married. On May 29, 1968, Harris, then twenty-two years old and a former Stanford University student body president, was sentenced to three years in prison for refusing induction into the armed forces. To avoid media coverage, the government finally took him into custody July 16, 1969—the day the Apollo 11 moonshot started. In December 1969 Joan gave birth to their son, Gabriel, and after a few months continued to travel around the country singing and expounding her nonviolent philosophy, while her husband served his sentence.[12]

The shock of David's incarceration seemed to produce a

new Joan Baez, Most people noticed that she cut her long hair (once a distinct trademark), but her mental change was far more striking. The uncertain, often petulant folksinger suddenly became a confident, aggressive extemporaneous speaker. Her appearance on national television talk shows was a good example. As a guest on the now defunct "Alan Burke Show" in 1967, Baez had been browbeaten and put on the defensive by the generally shallow Burke. The following year, when she and David appeared on "The Les Crane Show," Joan had sung songs, but let David do most of the talking. However, a year later, on "The Dick Cavett Show," a month after David's imprisonment, she completely confounded Cavett's attempt at witty superficiality with a moving and articulate explanation of her pacifist philosophy. Joan so outpointed the usually glib, if not profound, Cavett that the next day Howard K. Smith was moved to use the commentary portion of his nightly news show to respond to Baez's arguments. Smith called Joan "one of our high-income revolutionaries," and dismissed her as an idealist who naively believed that revolution would bring perfection out of ruins. Smith contended that America was a middle-class country which abhorred revolution and that the path to progress was one of slow "precinct work" in elections and legislation.[13]

There was also a noticeable change in Baez's concert appearances. She insisted that tickets to her performances could cost no more than two dollars, and she developed a more commanding stage presence. In September 1970 she demonstrated her new confidence at a concert in Sopot, Poland. After singing "Blowin' in the Wind" and a Beatle song, she explained (through a translator) why David was in prison and then sang one of her own compositions, which she dedicated to the young Poles who she felt were in the same position as American youths—"hitchhiking but with no place to go." Afterward at a press conference, when asked about America's "sickness," she replied, "America is not the sickest but the biggest. If Poland was as big as America, she might be just as destructive." The translator omitted the last part of her answer.[14] Back home she was now considered more dangerous. On February 3, 1971, Miami, Florida, officials refused to allow her to give a college-sponsored concert in the city's Marine Stadium, arguing that her appearance might present a "problem of crowd control."[15] Yet she was never a direct political threat. People were generally unwilling to hear her speak unless she also sang. During her February 1971 tour, for example, she drew 7,000 people to a paid concert, but only 400 showed up for a free political talk.[16]

David Harris was paroled on March 15, 1971, after serving twenty months of his three-year sentence. Meanwhile, Joan had been in good form on talk shows. Upon her return to "The Dick Cavett Show," the somewhat chastened host introduced her as "the leading lady of American folk music." Despite this respectful introduction, Baez's manner was very condescending. She obviously resented Dick's mild attempts at levity and treated him as a somewhat backward child. The conversation centered on prisons and Joan observed that incarceration was educative. Since bank robbers came out of prison better bank robbers, she argued, "If you go into prison a pacifist, you come out a better pacifist." Cavett later noted that prisons were bad, but asked Joan what society should do with serious criminals, like murderers. She replied, "If you talk about serious murderers, they are not in our jails, they are running nations." A month later Baez faced a generally hostile audience on the "David Frost Show" although Frost himself was sympathetic. Here she adopted a lecture stance and noted that though people were afraid of chaos if they did not have government, our government was chaotic. She argued that Americans were "disciplined to the point where" they could not even think, and thus were insulated from "the Cambodian mother whose child has been burned." Joan's solution was to work outside the system to build a society that did not "corrupt people." She felt it was impossible to reform the system itself and when asked to sing a song that reflected her present mood, she sang, "Heaven Help Us All."[17] Critics could point out that Baez still came up with simplistic, one-dimensional answers, but there was a new, strangely effective power in her verbal arguments. The often shy folksinger had suddenly become a rather charismatic agitator. Looking back, it is ironic that Bob Dylan, now perhaps the most reclusive of the pop singers, criticized Baez for her passiveness and lack of relevance. In 1962 Dylan observed:

> It ain't nothin' just to walk around and sing . . . you have to step out a little, right? Take Joanie, man, she's still singing about Mary Hamilton. I mean where's that at? She's walked around on picket lines, she's got all kinds of feeling, so why ain't she steppin' out?[18]

Although by 1965 Dylan had completely rejected activism or even relevance and had in fact dropped out physically, Joan did indeed step out. Other serious and gifted folksingers like Judy Collins sang Malvina Reynolds's song, "It Isn't Nice," about how it wasn't nice "to block the doorways" and "go to jail." Baez actually sat in the doorways and went to jail. While other former topical singers turned to catchy top-ten ballads and cashed in on television guest appearances, Joan put out an average of one record per year, sang college-circuit concerts, and invested most of her money in causes like her own Institute. In an era when credibility became the magic word, it is not hard to understand why Joan Baez's star was in the ascendancy.

Joan's personal philosophy of nonviolence has become increasingly sophisticated. Her two major influences have been Ira Sandperl, a veteran of West Coast pacifist crusades, and her husband. In 1964 Joan asked Sandperl to tutor her on the philosophy of nonviolence and the lessons turned into The Institute for the Study of Nonviolence. Sandperl, now fifty-one years old, has remained the guiding influence behind the Institute. Founded in 1965, the school began to focus its energy on specific goals after 1970. Brief workshops and pacifist philosophy remain the heart of the Institute's program. However, the communal living, an integral part of the workshops, has recently been applied locally through experiments with land and food cooperatives and political action groups.[19] David Harris's influence on Baez has largely been one of emphasis. His philosophy (set forth in his book *Goliath*) is hazy, but he styles himself an organizer rather than a preacher. Joan's new aggressiveness can be traced to her husband's vigorous brand of organized pacifism.[20] Joan probably summed up her pacifist outlook in the following passage from *Daybreak:*

> The problem isn't communism. The problem is consensus. There's a consensus out that it's OK to kill when your government decides who to kill. If you kill inside the country you get in trouble. If you kill outside the country, right time, right season, latest enemy, you get a medal. There are about 130 nation-states, and each of them thinks it's a swell idea to bump off all the rest because he is more important. The pacifist thinks there is only one tribe. Three billion members. They come first. We think there are more decent and intelligent ways of settling differences. And man had better start investigating these other possibilities because if he doesn't, then by mistake or by design, he will probably kill off the whole damn race.[21]

At various times Baez has stressed that music alone was not enough for her. In 1970 she observed that if she did not stand up for life in deed as well as in song, all those beautiful sounds were "irrelevant to the only real question of this century: How do we stop men from murdering each other."[22] Nevertheless, for millions of Americans she is her music. Divorced from her songs, she is incomplete. For Joan personally, the music is both hope and catharsis.

"To sing," Joan wrote, "is to love and to affirm, to fly and soar, to coast into the hearts of the people who listen, to tell them that life is to live, that love is there, that nothing is a promise, but that beauty exists, and must be hunted for and found."[23] If her songs do give her wings, it is not apparent at her concerts. Baez's singing has a solemnity which is independent of her material and quickly transferred to the audience. People do not sway to her music, and handclapping would seem ludicrous. The fragile nature of her lyrics encourages people to protect them with a hushed silence. Her recent concerts are considerably looser because of the larger, less intimate audiences and her new outgoing style.

The earlier concerts were rather mystical. I first heard Baez perform in November 1962 at the University of Illinois. Dressed in a plain skirt and blouse, she walked onto the stage of an auditorium filled with 1,500 students, sat down on a stool, and without a word started playing. After some forty minutes of songs, punctuated only by brief introductions and the dedication of one song to Pete Seeger, she walked off at intermission without any indication she was returning. The second half of her program was a copy of the first. She ended her concert with one encore and a simple "Thank you, goodnight." Few faulted her lack of showmanship. Baez's voice seemed completely independent of the frail figure on the stage. At one point she quietly commanded the audience, "Sing this one with me"; and the assembly sang along in whispered voices as if they were in church. It is easy to understand her magnetic effect at Woodstock in August 1969, when at 2 A.M. she stood, noticeably pregnant, singing to a dreamy sea of flower children.

On her recordings, Baez's voice has recently lost some of its magic, being rather overpowered by electronic sidemen and subverted by echo chambers and sound-on-sound arrangements. Yet periodically, as the accompaniment fades, her voice breaks through, all the stronger in contrast. Balance has been the strong point of Joan's albums. She never sang one type of song; and thus even her hard-core protest songs were seldom tedious.

Nevertheless, Joan always had critics. In regard to her early albums, *Little Sandy Review*, headquarters for "folkier than thou" criticism, conceded that Baez was "perhaps the most thrilling young voice of our time," but sadly concluded that her vocal gifts were "too rich and too grandiose to carry the simplicity of the humble folk song." When the traditional singer like Woody Guthrie or Leadbelly sang a folksong, the *LSR* reviewers argued, it described "the basic nature of his land and people." Baez could only describe herself, for in "molding a song to her own powerful personality" she destroyed it. Joan did not lack defenders. After reviewing Baez's first album, the *LSR* reviewers noted that her many fervent fans had requested that they "quit picking on Joan" and "go back to beating" their "grandmothers with old Library of Congress albums."[24] Likewise, Baez's 1969 dual album of Bob Dylan songs, *Any Day Now*, was panned by "Dylanologist" Alan Weberman, because "Joanie's sweet soprano voice" could not express the heavy contemptuous sarcasm of many of Dylan's songs.[25]

Yet Baez's albums, like Dylan's, resist generalizations. Unlike Dylan's, they show steady growth. Joan's first three albums contained largely traditional folksongs, with the exception of Malvina Reynold's low-key protest song, "What Have They Done to the Rain." In 1962 her fourth album reflected Dylan's influence. She sang two of his songs, including a long pacifist ballad, "With God on Our Side." Her civil rights concern was represented by the "Battle Hymn of the Republic" and and audience participation rendition of "We Shall Overcome." Every song on the third and fourth albums was taped in concert. Her fifth album, in 1963, was a very mixed bag indeed. Along with one of Dylan's personal laments, "It Ain't Me Babe," there were Phil Ochs's social environmental ballad, "There But For Fortune," a Johnny Cash song, the usual traditional songs, and "Birmingham Sunday," Richard Fariña's memorial to black children killed in a church bombing. Her next offering, in 1965, was much the same with a little more emphasis on Dylan. Four of Bob's songs appeared, including the title song, "Farewell Angelina," and his older warning of nuclear war, "A Hard Rain's A-Gonna Fall." After deciding not to release an album of rock-type songs in 1966, she replaced it with a Christmas album.[26] Joan supposedly vetoed the rock music because she had read that Gandhi "rejected art if it didn't represent truth—if it didn't elevate the soul." Rock-'n-roll was fun, but it failed to meet Gandhi's standards. "I still like to sing it sometimes," she said, "but it doesn't represent what I feel."[27]

As usual, her 1967 album gave mixed indications of her real feelings. Titled *Joan*, the record had full orchestra accompaniment, and contained two songs Baez co-authored, "North" and "Saigon Bride"—the latter a rather profound antiwar ballad. *Baptism*, her next album, was a real change of pace and commercially her least successful venture. It featured a wide assortment of poems, both spoken and sung, centering on the sanctity of life. In 1969 there followed her dual-record set of Dylan songs and a homey album, dedicated to her imprisoned husband. The latter two records were made in Nashville and followed Bob Dylan's move toward a country-and-western emphasis. Like Dylan, Baez has continued to use many of the excellent Nashville-based sidemen for accompaniment.

One Day at a Time, her 1970 entry, included her first individual compositions, "Sweet Sir Galahad" and "A Song for David"—both intensely personal and remarkably melodic ballads. The same year Vanguard released a two-record anthology of Joan's last ten years of songs. In 1971 Joan Baez reached maturity as a writer-performer with her dual-record album, *Blessed Are*. Baez wrote nine of its twenty songs. Taken as a whole they indicated her considerable promise as a writer. Joan's ballads, like her prose in *Daybreak*, are very uneven, but show flashes of brilliance both in melody and lyrics. *Blessed Are* contained very diverse songs; yet, whereas the diversity of earlier records stemmed from her eclectic approach to music, the later mix seemed purposeful. Joan has steadily become more tolerant, and increasingly her songs have reflected the common conditions of all men. On *Blessed Are* she sang sympathetically about a Confederate soldier in Robbie Robertson's "The Night They Drove Old Dixie Down," about a "red-neck Georgia farmboy" in Mickey Newbury's "San Francisco Mabel Joy," and about middle-class Southern landholders in her own "Outside the Nashville City Limits." Add to these her renditions of Kris Kristofferson's "Help Me Make It Through the Night," Lennon-McCartney's "Let It Be," Ron Miller's "Heaven Help Us All," and her own title song, "Blessed Are," and you have a package that pointedly stresses universal togetherness.

It appeared that Baez's art and politics were finally coming together. The best indication of this was her 1972 album, *Come from the Shadows*. On the cover was a photo of

an elderly couple involved in a protest demonstration—
holding hands with one hand and showing the peace sign
with the other—while two helmeted policemen stand by. On
the back cover Baez asked citizens "to take some risks. Stop
paying war taxes, refuse the armed forces . . . give up the
nation-state, share your money . . . in short, sisters and
brothers, arm up with love and come from the shadows."

Of the album's twelve songs, Baez wrote six. Her songs
included "Prison Trilogy," a protest against our prisons
which ends by asking help to "raze the prisons to the
ground," and "Bangladesh," a ballad describing the slaugh-
ter of innocent people on the altar of nationalism. Another
Baez composition, "All the Weary Mothers of the Earth,"
looked forward to a millennial day when all the mothers,
farmers, and workers on earth will rest in a peaceful world.
Her most interesting ballad was "To Bobby," a rather evident
though not explicit appeal to Bob Dylan, asking him to
rejoin the protest movement. The song accused Bobby of
leaving the protesters "marching on the road" when the
struggle was "barely at its start." One line commented that
"no one could say it" like Bobby "said it"; the others would
just "try and then forget it." The last verse noted that Baez
and her associates continued to march in the streets "with
little victories and big defeats" and still reserved a place for
the unidentified Bobby Rounding out the album's songs were
Mimi Fariña's "In the Quiet Morning," a memorial to Janis
Joplin; a World War Two ballad, "The Partisan," here
dedicated to Melina Mercouri and those suffering under "the
current Greek dictatorship"; and John Lennon's hit, "Imagine," a call for one-world socialism. *Come from the Shadows* was the most explicitly political of Baez's albums, and
though it was somewhat gushy and polemic in spots, Joan's
own compositions maintained the promise of her earlier
songs. The trend continued with her 1973 album, *Where Are
You Now, My Son?*, which devoted the entire back side to a
long ballad "written, spoken, and sung by" Joan about "the
eleven days of bombing" she had experienced in Hanoi,
North Vietnam, during her 1972 Christmas visit. The album

also contained eight personal songs, of which she wrote four. On the back cover, Baez had written a letter about her Hanoi trip which concluded, "The war in Indochina is not yet over, and the war against violence has barely begun."[28]

As Baez has increased the scope and control of her music, her musical identity has become less important. Once she was a pacifist folksinger, now she sees herself as a folksinger pacifist. However, most Americans see Joan as a celebrity. Her celebrity status is evidenced by the regular appearance of her name in the "People" sections of *Newsweek* and *Time* and in daily syndicated gossip columns. It is further evidenced by the balloting for the Playboy Jazz & Pop Hall of Fame. In the latest poll, Baez placed thirteenth, right behind rock-star Frank Zappa and ahead of singer Barbra Streisand.[29] Thus, at first glance Joan appears to be an example of a twentieth-century celebrity type that historian Daniel Boorstin defined as a person who is famous "for his well-knownness."[30] Yet Baez is hardly a classic celebrity. She was not suddenly created by the media's need for instant cultural heroes. It was her deeds rather than her image that had changed over the years. Baez's celebrity status made her beliefs and actions newsworthy, but her activities usually threatened her professional career.

Moreover, Joan felt that celebrities have a responsibility. In 1967 when Bob Dylan was at the height of his popularity, and Baez's career was somewhat in eclipse, Joan noted:

> The kids idealize Dylan more than me. For that reason I think he should help them more, not play up to their negative feelings. What they want to hear is that nothing matters; and in a way that's what his newer songs tell them. I say just the opposite; I believe everything matters, and you have to take a stand.[31]

Unlike Dylan and other rock stars, Baez had neither the attitudes nor life-style to endear her to the counter culture. True, she was frankly bisexual, condoned premarital sex, and advocated trial marriage (and had practiced what she preached), but she urged discipline and commitment and was rather puritanical about drugs. In 1968 she admitted a "total dislike" for liquor and cigarettes, as well as marijuana or other drugs. "I get high as a cloud on one sleeping pill," Joan observed, "if that's what it means to get high; and it's not a whole lot different from what I feel like on a fall day in New England, or listening to the Fauré Requiem."[32] Also, Baez has steadily drawn criticism from the young left for her negative attitude toward various black power movements and women's liberation groups. Joan's position is based on the belief that people must concentrate on what they have in common rather than what sets them apart. She feels that power ultimately subverts and corrupts those who gain it. For Baez, even Martin Luther King's nonviolent movement was faulty, since it sought narrow changes by pressuring government. Joan's hero is Gandhi, who never asked for power, but "assumed that the power was the people's" and brought change by asking the people, rather than the government, to act.[33]

Not surprisingly, Baez has also been attacked from the right. In 1966 David Noebel charged that Joan's Institute was a Marxist-oriented front that trained "musclebound toughs" for group disruptions. Noebel also noted that in 1962 the two biggest donors to the United Nations were Nelson Rockefeller and Joan Baez (who gave $1,361.60); and that Joan's father held "down one of the highest paid jobs in the UNESCO Secretariat."[34] More importantly, in 1967 cartoonist Al Capp introduced a character into his "Li'l Abner" strip named "Joanie Phoanie." Miss Phoanie was a long-haired folksinger who collected $10,000 a concert, refused to pay taxes, and spent most of her spare time organizing sordid, anti-American demonstrations. Joan's defenders pointed out that Capp had made his fortune distorting and maligning the image of Appalachian whites, so his treatment of Baez was a logical extension of his work.[35]

Largely because of the controversy that has surrounded her, Baez has been a cultural hero of youth throughout the decade. Earlier, however, she was only a model of style. In 1962, for example, *Time* suggested how to look like a female "folknik": "It is not absolutely essential to have hair hanging to the waist—but it helps. Other aids: no lipstick, flat shoes, a guitar."[36] *Time* really described how to look like Joan Baez. At present, a cursory glance at any group of teenage girls (or perhaps boys also) quickly indicates that the style Baez picked up in the bohemian corners of Cambridge and later helped popularize is now everywhere triumphant. Millions of youths now dress in long hair and ostentatious poverty. Joan does not cherish her part in the style revolution, since her message was never explicitly in her life-style. As early as 1961, Baez felt that she had "a lot to say," but added, "I don't know how to say it so I just sing it."[37] Later, no doubt, she felt that it was not enough to sing it or say it, so she did it. If Marshall McLuhan is any guide, she is on the right track. For if "the medium is the message," surely the singer must, in part, be the lyrics.

Baez has come a long way intellectually, but her answers to social problems often remain naive, hopeful, and vague (or as social scientists would say, without empirical foundation). Joan probably realizes this much more in her new-found maturity. She has admitted that she cannot explain her "innermost convictions." For her, it is enough to say, "A tree is known by its fruits. People see how I manage myself, and maybe from that they can see what I'm about."[38] Perhaps Joan Baez is a fake—the brainchild of a brilliant public relations man, a pseudo–protest singer who chose to become commercial by being noncommercial. Perhaps her activities are really sublimations for personal conflicts she only dimly perceives. Perhaps her vision of a nonviolent world is based on untenable assumptions about human nature. In any case, I read the record of her life as indicating that she came by her convictions honestly—indeed, that her beliefs were rationally shaped by her odyssey through the turbulent 1960s.

Baez has clearly been cast in the hero's role. In 1971, in Antioch College's annual poll of their freshmen to determine what prominent persons of recent history the students most admired, Joan Baez placed eleventh, right behind John Kennedy. Women's liberation notwithstanding, she was the first woman on the list. Gandhi ranked first and Martin Luther King second; others among the top ten were Malcolm X, Albert Schweitzer, Ralph Nader, Cesar Chavez, and Pablo Picasso.[39] Baez was indeed in august company. However, perhaps her strong showing was not too surprising. Increasingly, Joan appeared wherever the action was. Marching in the streets, on television talk shows, in daily news dispatches, or singing the title song in a movie about Sacco and Vanzetti, she seemed a natural symbol of the era.

Perhaps in no other decade could a female pacifist become a cultural hero, or a folksinger become a symbol for American youth. Like Joan of Arc, Baez inspired by example and symbolized innocence and purity. For many, Joan Baez fulfilled the perennial quest for an individual pure in heart who could not be bought. Too volatile and profane to be a serious candidate for sainthood, Baez has nevertheless acquired a saintly image. Although she has long since written off the Berkeley Free Speech Movement as an "unviolent" movement (ready to switch to violence to obtain its goals), as opposed to a truly "nonviolent" movement, her part in the Berkeley turmoil was a good example of her charisma. "Have love as you do this thing," Joan told a Berkeley mob, "and it will succeed." Later, *Time* reported that a thousand undergraduates had "stormed" the administration building "marching behind their Joan of Arc, who was wearing a jeweled crucifix."[40] At first glance it seemed odd to compare the peaceful Baez to the warrior-maid of France; but then Baez does insist on describing herself as a "nonviolent soldier." And on "The Les Crane Show," she admitted once instructing a crowd of protesters, "Be nonviolent or I'll kill you!" And so I choose to see her as "a pacifist St. Joan"—on a white horse, without armor, guitar (rather than lance) in hand—riding at the head of a nonviolent army.

7: Bob Dylan:
Beyond Left and Right

*I don't believe in anything. No, why should I believe
in anything? I don't see anything to believe in.*[1]
—Bob Dylan

That Bob Dylan, who did not "believe in anything,"
became one of the most universally admired idols of American youth during the 1960s tells us much about the youthful
ethos of that turbulent decade. Perhaps Dylan's most
famous song was "The Times They Are A Changin'";
certainly his earliest hit was "Blowin' in the Wind." Fittingly
enough, throughout the 1960s Dylan changed with the
times and blew in the wind. The question is, did he personally alter the times or stir the currents of change? Most
commentators quickly agree that he did, but Bob himself has
consistently answered that he had never tried to change
anything; doubted that he had changed anything; hoped that
he had not changed anything, and in any event just plain did
not care.[2]

Dylan's constant disclaiming of social influence was not
a sign of modesty, but an integral part of both his outlook

and mystique. It was important that Bob not care about what people thought about himself, his influence, or his songs. Dylan saw himself as a free, creative, existential spirit in a society filled with the personal and public prisons of civilization. To care was to bind yourself, to be a leader was to be a prisoner. "Don't follow leaders," Bob advised in a song, "watch parking meters." Dylan felt that you did not have to be "a Weatherman" "to know which way the wind" blew. Thus Dylan, who feared becoming a preacher, preached that caring, leading, and following were obsolete in the chaotic, absurd 1960s. For many the decade seemed to provide object lessons in Dylan's philosophy—from Vietnam to the Nixon administration.

Many young people found Dylan's supercool both heroic and inviting. Perhaps Bob's existential coolness invited involvement and participation for the same reasons Marshall McLuhan suggested that the"cool" medium of television was involving. Both Dylan and TV were relatively low in definition. One had to work very hard to get the total picture of a television scene from the rough scanning lines or to understand a Dylan song from the lyric's ragged, poetic phrases.[3] Indeed, as Dylan turned his back on the outside world and moved steadily inward, it was harder and harder to trace his intellectual path through his songs. Eastern mystics and nineteenth-century American transcendentalists such as Emerson and Thoreau had long argued that the only place to go was in. Likewise, the American bohemian beats had followed Jack Kerouac and Allen Ginsberg on an inward journey in the hip 1950s. However, Dylan was easily the first popular singer to make the trip, and he became a cultural hero precisely because he took that route. American youths increasingly wanted mystique and charisma, and Dylan provided both.

There was little in Dylan's childhood background that suggested either charisma or mystique. Born Robert Zimmerman in Duluth, Minnesota, in 1941, Bob grew up in Hibbing, Minnesota, an iron-mining center close to the Canadian border. His father, Abe Zimmerman, owned an appliance store. Bob was part of a typical, middle-class,

Jewish-American family. It is difficult to take Judaism matter-of-factly in America. One either embraces it or rejects it. Dylan clearly rejected his Jewishness along with his name and a host of middle-class trappings. In effect Zimmerman the small-town Jew became Dylan the poetic, road-weary WASP. There were ample reasons to encourage a metamorphosis. Hibbing, no doubt, had the same effect on Dylan that another small Minnesota town, Sauk Centre, had on novelist Sinclair Lewis. In his novel, *Main Street,* Lewis described his hometown as follows:

> It is an unimaginatively standardized background, a sluggish-ness of speech and manners, a rigid ruling of the spirit by the desire to appear respectable. It is contentment—the content-ment of the quiet dead. . . . It is dullness made God.

Dylan's response to Hibbing was to run away from home, according to his testimony, when he was "10, 12, 13, 15, 15½, 17, and 18." He recalled that he was "caught an' brought back all but once."[4] But perhaps Bob never really escaped Hibbing until he legally changed his name to Bob Dylan on August 9, 1962. (Bob has never admitted that he took his name from poet Dylan Thomas, but most of Bob's friends have always thought that was the origin.)

Before he got away for good, Dylan went through the conventional small-town upbringing. He moved uneventfully through the public school system, worked at his father's appliance store as a teenager, and impressed his high school classmates as a quiet lone wolf. Unlike many recent radicals, Dylan did not have a happy, secure youth. Activists like Jerry Rubin and Tom Hayden were content as teenagers and radicalized in college, where they identified their interests with those of the lower class. They found their purpose suddenly, like Saul on the road. Dylan, however, grew up alienated from both family and society. Whereas Rubin and Hayden admired their middle-class, hard-working parents, Dylan rejected his father as a stock Jewish bourgeois store-keeper. Indeed, Hibbing society no doubt agreed with Bob's view of his father, and Bob in turn rejected his community even more than his family.

Yet Hibbing had its advantages as Dylan's foil. The city

was largely Catholic and overwhelmingly square; Bob was Jewish and culturally restless. He remained outside every group, young or adult. His earliest girl friend, Echo Hellstrom, remembered him as an eternal loner. He mixed with the rock-and-roll crowd in high school, but was not one of them. He had a motorcycle and black leather jacket, but was never accepted by the black-booted bike crowd.[5] For one thing, Dylan wrote poetry, and this pushed him further to the periphery of his peer group. At the edges of American society, Bob saw more than most. His detachment furnished him with his artistic perspective and nourished his creativity. One could argue that Bob spent the first half of his life reacting to being a Jew in a small Minnesota town and the second half reacting to his growing role as a musical messiah for America's developing counter culture. Throughout his professional career he would feel uneasy near the center of society and threatened by the absorbing power of affluent America. He would work hard at keeping his distance and remaining reclusive. From Hibbing to New York to Nashville, Dylan instinctively sensed that American society sought to shape one into what Herbert Marcuse described as a "one-dimensional man," unable to see beyond social norms. Dylan had self-consciously escaped the mass American experience and thus retained the poetic vision that kept him one step ahead of the trends. Increasingly, it became clear that his power lay in staying on the edge and looking in, rather than being at the center and looking out. Like Thoreau at Walden, Dylan had his own, peculiar "angle of vision."

Unlike Thoreau, Dylan was never a hermit, even at Hibbing. Mass media made it possible to receive all the mass social experiences without being there. You could live in your own world and at your leisure take in electronic signals from the outside. Perhaps Dylan was even shaped by the primitive, tribal nature of television that Marshall McLuhan first suggested. In any case, Dylan was certainly affected by the James Dean, lone-wolf mystique emanating from Hollywood. Later Dylan would often be seen as a Jewish James

Dean. Dean, like Dylan, was a restless small-town vagabond who rejected establishment America. No doubt Dylan was also influenced by the beat philosophy reflected in Jack Kerouac's *On the Road,* published in 1955. Yet music was Dylan's primary emotional oasis during his teenage years. If it were not, Dylan might easily have become a writer or an artist.

Bob's family could afford a piano and Dylan played it without lessons from the age of eight. As a teenager he taught himself guitar and harmonica. He learned to play both instruments simultaneously with the neck-brace, harmonica-holder style he would later make famous. Hibbing was hardly a center of American music, yet radio and recordings brought the latest trends in a steady wave. Starting with country-and-western music, Dylan worked his way through black rhythm-and-blues, and eventually folk music—all through the courtesy of disc jockeys and the local record shops. Meanwhile, the rock-and-roll revolution of the middle 1950s had hit Hibbing, and the sounds of Bill Haley, Little Richard, and Elvis Presley captured Dylan's fancy. As a high school performer, Bob played rock, but by the time he graduated he had lost himself in the new folk renaissance centered around the songs of Woody Guthrie. The Guthrie-oriented folk crowd were often radicals and activists as well as musicians, and for Dylan this put them on a somewhat higher plane than the merely musically rebellious rock stars. Dylan now found his earliest vocation as a young interpreter of Guthrie songs.

Guthrie's style had an obvious appeal for a young man aching to hit the road. Whereas Woody had drifted around the country to escape small-town depression, Dylan adopted Guthrie to escape small-town monotony. Not yet musically skilled enough to go forward, Dylan went back into depression America and emerged with a classic hard-traveling mentality. The Guthrie influence would pervade Dylan's music from his high school graduation in 1959 until he turned to amplified music in 1965. The gruff voice, Southern rural phrases, talking blues, dungaree uniform, and understated bandstand humor were pure Guthrie. Even Bob's life-style was similar to Woody's, with one important difference. Guthrie drifted from town to town and from situation to situation the length and breadth of the country, but Dylan was always a very specialized urban drifter. Bob too never knew where he would spend the night, but he moved only from Minneapolis to Chicago to New York and then only in the bohemian, folk-oriented sections of those cities. A folk club in Chicago was little different from one in New York. Whereas Guthrie's music reflected his life, Dylan's music was his only interest, and Bob traveled only from one musical experience to another.

Before totally losing himself in music, Dylan briefly sampled college life. In September 1959 he enrolled at the University of Minnesota and lived at a Jewish fraternity house. He lasted six months before dissolving into the beat subculture around the campus. Bob quickly picked up the rumpled bohemian look and mannerisms and for the first time sang under the name Bob Dylan at a Minneapolis coffeehouse. In "Dinkytown," the Greenwich Village of Minneapolis, Bobby Zimmerman disappeared and along with him his Hibbing past. The emerging, phoenixlike Dylan was a strange amalgam of 1930s-style Guthrieism and 1950s-style bohemianism. Dylan was to become one of the living bridges between beat bohemianism and the radical counter culture.

Late in 1960, Bob pointed himself toward Mecca. After a short stop in Chicago he traveled to New York City. There stood the "Village," and there also lay Woody Guthrie, in the last stages of a terminal illness and confined to a state hospital. Bob quickly indulged his dreams. He became a bona fide Greenwich Village resident and established an apparently warm relationship with Guthrie after visiting him in the hospital. More importantly, Dylan immersed himself in the close folk music culture that blossomed in Village coffeehouses. Dylan soaked up the variety of folk styles like a sponge. The main reason for his success, however, was a quick acceptance by the elder folk professionals.

Singers like Dave Van Ronk and Paul Clayton were in awe of the baby-faced Dylan, who sang like Guthrie, talked like a grizzled Okie, and lived and ate music. Bob had a small but professional fan club long before he had a public one and this obviously gave him confidence. For some time, folk music would be an esoteric art for small specialized audiences, and the most important audience was the performers themselves.

Within three months after he arrived, Dylan was playing regularly in small Village coffeehouses, culminating in a two-week stand at Gerde's Folk City, center stage for New York folkniks. During the next six months he rounded out his coterie of Village professionals, met Suze Rotolo, a girl he would be stormily attached to for the next few years, and finally appeared on a record. In September 1961 Dylan agreed to play harmonica on folksinger Carolyn Hester's first album for Columbia records. John Hammond, Columbia's chief folk talent scout, immediately sensed Dylan's genius and signed him to a generous contract. Later that month Bob opened another stand at Gerde's Folk City and John Shelton, folk critic for the *New York Times*, brought him to public attention with a glowing review of his performance. Now stardom was only a matter of time and timing. Folk music and especially protest music was coming into its own. Joan Baez had just put out her first album. Protest writers like Phil Ochs and Tom Paxton had just moved into the Village, while early in 1962 *Broadside* magazine was founded as a showcase for protest music. In February 1962 Bob's first album came out, and in April 1962 Dylan took command of the whole scene by writing "Blowin' in the Wind," his low-key civil rights and pacifist ballad. From that moment till he stopped writing topical songs in 1964, Dylan was undisputed leader of the folk-protest genre. He was still not a public idol. That distinction would await his move into rock music, yet he was an inspiration to the many young folk writers and performers who followed his lead.[6]

Dylan found life at the top hazardous and demanding. As a protest leader he was expected to ride the tides of politics and activism. It was fairly easy to oblige as long as civil rights and the arms race were fresh issues, but today's protests quickly became yesterday's clichés. Dylan became increasingly uncomfortable putting the obvious into poetic phrases. Bob's first album, *Bob Dylan*, consisted of traditional folksongs such as "House of the Rising Sun," contemporary blues such as Ric von Schmidt's "Baby Let Me Follow You Down," and two of Dylan's own songs—"Talking New York" and "Song to Woody." His second and third albums, *The Freewheelin' Bob Dylan* (released in May 1963) and *The Times They Are A-Changin'* (January 1964), represented the high tide of his protest music. Each album was split between topical protest songs like "Masters of War," "With God on Our Side," and "Only a Pawn in Their Game" and personal ballads like "Don't Think Twice" and "Restless Farewell," both of which concerned Dylan's stormy relationship with Suze Rotolo.[7]

Meanwhile Dylan rounded out his liberal credentials in fine style. In May 1963 he was invited to appear on the Ed Sullivan Show, but refused when CBS censors would not allow him to sing his controversial song, "Talking John Birch Society Blues." Bob met Joan Baez at the Monterey Folk Festival in the spring of 1963, and Dylan and Baez headlined the prestigious Newport Folk Festival that summer. In 1964 Dylan was featured in *Time* and *Life* profiles. His ballad, "The Times They Are A-Changin'," became a symbol of the newly-discovered generation gap as well as one of the year's most popular songs.[8] But Dylan decisively turned away from protest and activism in 1964. In August 1963 he had sung at Martin Luther King's massive freedom march in Washington, but two weeks after John F. Kennedy's assassination in November Bob cut himself off from civil rights and general activism in a typically hazy way. Dylan gave a distraught, babbling speech in New York, while accepting the Thomas Paine award of the Emergency Civil Liberties Committee for his civil rights work. Dylan rather incoherently proclaimed that old people should retire from activism and enjoy themselves, since political reform was hopeless and the civil rights advocates were largely hypocritical. As Dylan put it:

They talk about Negroes and they talk about black and white.
. . . Man, I just don't seen any colors at all when I look out.. . . .
There's no black and white, left and right, to me anymore.
There's only up and down, and down is very close to the
ground. And I'm trying to go up without thinking of anything
trivial such as politics.[9]

Dylan's career as a protest singer had come to a sudden
halt, though it was years before many people would believe
it. Indeed, a few of the faithful would continually appeal to
him to rejoin the movement for change. Dylan now struck
out in several directions. He was getting involved with drugs,
his relationship with Suze Rotolo had deteriorated further,
and he took off on a cross-country auto trip with his personal
entourage of friends. In 1964 Dylan also became more interested in rock music, especially the British variety represented
by the Beatles. Bob did a British concert tour in May 1964 and
had a chance to get even closer to the new music. All these
changes were evident in his new album, *Another Side of Bob
Dylan*, released in August 1964. Gone were the protest songs.
In their place was "Back Pages," a ballad recounting his
erring protesting ways and explaining that while he was
"much older then," he was "younger than that now." Other
songs of personal freedom included "Chimes of Freedom," "I
Shall Be Free," and his classic "It Ain't Me Babe." Filling out
the album were songs about his personal relationship with
Suze Rotolo such as "All I Really Want to Do" and "I Don't
Believe You." Meanwhile Bob was doing concerts and introducing the first of his really abstract, free verse ballads like
"Gates of Eden" and "Mr. Tambourine Man." In March 1965
these latter two songs appeared with others like them on his
album *Bringing It All Back Home*. The new songs were filled
with bold impressionist images and mystical themes. They
could be interpreted in hundreds of ways and indeed they still
are. The album was clearly the product of Dylan's split with
old friends, his drug experiences, and the general jolt of his
becoming a superstar. Dylan moved into his private mixed-
up world and as always the songs faithfully reflected his state.

Now the stage was set for Dylan the folk star to become
Dylan the rock star. English musicians had already produced
crude folk-rock, but when an American rock group, The

Turtles, made Dylan's "Mr. Tambourine Man" into a hit, folk-rock had really arrived. On *Bringing It All Back Home*, Bob had used electric instruments for the entire first side, and hereafter he steadily moved into electronic rock style.

Throughout 1965 Dylan made concert appearances with Joan Baez, including a tour of Britain which later became the subject of a film, *Don't Look Back*. Evidently Dylan and Baez had been lovers for the past year, but Bob's move away from social commitment and into rock music drove a wedge between them that continued to widen. By the end of his English tour, Bob and Joan had ended their relationship both emotionally and professionally. Shortly thereafter, back in New York, Bob met his future wife, Sarah Lowndes, for the first time.

In July 1965 Dylan made his final break with the folk music traditionalists. More precisely, it was forced on him. At the Newport Folk Festival he was booed off the stage when he appeared in mod clothing, with an electric guitar, to sing one of his latest abstract songs, "Like A Rolling Stone." He returned with folk guitar to deliver a few of his older songs. However, it was probably no accident that he started with his farewell ballad, "It's All Over Now Baby Blue." It was indeed all over between Dylan and the folk faithful. Undaunted, Dylan formed his own rock back-up band and launched a hugely successful concert tour in which he played rock for half the program and folk ballads for the remainder. In August 1965 his new rock album, *Highway 61 Revisited*, was released and well received. The following May an even wilder collection of Dylan rock tunes appeared in a double-album format titled *Blonde on Blonde*.

Dylan had obviously made it by 1966. He was the biggest thing in music. Yet fame had taken its toll. He broke off relations with several old friends and became more peevish with the hordes of reporters trying to use him for copy. Evidently he also became more dependent on drugs and he underwent noticeable physical deterioration. The gaunt Dylan who stared out from the cover of the *Blonde on Blonde* album seemed only the shell of the always thin, yet robust, younger Dylan. Perhaps inevitably and even luckily, Dylan's hectic upward and downward spiral was broken by a serious motorcycle accident that put him in the hospital for weeks and forced an introspection that would change his life-style and of course his music. He had just finished a long grinding concert tour that took him across the United States to Hawaii, Australia, and finally Europe, before he returned to his home in Woodstock, New York. On July 30, near Woodstock, Dylan's motorcycle swerved and threw him to the pavement. He suffered a badly broken neck, a concussion, and lacerations.

In recuperating, Dylan retired from the world as a monk to a monastery. He remained isolated at his Woodstock home for nine months while people spread exaggerated rumors about his physical condition. Finally in May 1967 Bob gave an interview and made plans to resume his musical career. The following October he went to Nashville, Tennessee, to record an album that would be released in January 1968 as *John Wesley Harding*. The album songs showed a more subdued, spiritual Dylan. The music was only mildly electric, the folk tunes were simple, and the mood was quiet, yet the phrases were more mystical and existential than ever. The song titles, like "I Pity the Poor Immigrant," and "I Dreamed I Saw St. Augustine," as usual told little. The album was a critical success, but not an overwhelming financial success. Groups like the Beatles and Rolling Stones had clearly replaced Dylan in the rock world. Vietnam and the campus rebellion had run their own frenetic course while Bob lay meditating at Woodstock. The new Dylan came from another world and spoke about yet another world. Yet as always, for those tired of the present, Dylan had something new to offer, and as usual some argued that Bob's new lyrics were really coded, subtle protests about contemporary evils like the war.

Dylan was now a contented family man. He had secretly married Sarah Lowndes in November 1965, and in addition to her daughter (by a previous marriage), by 1968 Dylan had a son and daughter of his own. He continued to work at a slow, contented pace, restricting his concert appearances to a

Woody Guthrie memorial concert at Carnegie Hall. He finally taped another leisurely album in Nashville, late in 1968, that was released in April 1969 as *Nashville Skyline*. The Bob Dylan pictured on the album cover was a smiling country-and-western singer obviously at peace with the world. The album songs, like "Peggy Day," "Tonight I'll Be Staying Here With You," "Lay Lady Lay" (a runaway hit single), and "Country Pie," all registered contentment. In August 1969 Dylan returned to the concert scene with a low-key, but profitable ($75,000), appearance at the Isle of Wight Festival in Britain. The next summer Bob celebrated his new respectability by accepting an honorary Doctorate of Music from Princeton University. In the meantime he released a generally boring dual-album of older standards sung in his new easygoing and versatile voice style.

The album of standards, *Self-Portrait*, convinced many that Dylan had at last completely sold out and was on his way to becoming a younger Perry Como. However, in October 1970 Dylan surprised the critics by releasing a new album, *New Morning*, which was filled with harder-driving, more innovative songs that dramatically showed he had not lost his magic touch. The songs, like "If Not For You" and the title ballad, "New Morning," generally celebrated the mystery of life and were probing rather than critical, yet they continued the lyrical philosophical searching that Dylan had begun with *John Wesley Harding* after his accident. Clearly Dylan was not finished yet. If he was no longer the existential hero of the left, neither was he an emaciated Johnny Cash or a Tin Pan Alley performer.

Since 1971, Dylan has maintained the same low-key musical profile. Although the music industry has followed his lead into quieter, country-oriented rock music, Bob has hardly been a leader. Rather Dylan has been in semi-retirement. In 1974 a long-awaited new album, *Planet Waves*, appeared and a new cross-country and worldwide concert tour was organized. Both ventures offered nostalgia rather than new directions. They were a step back into the past rather than a step into the future. Indeed, the past continues to define the contemporary Bob Dylan. Those who swarmed to his recent concerts sought to capture themselves in the 1960s rather than to observe Dylan in the 1970s. Unlike any other performer Dylan had symbolized what it meant to be young and alienated in the 1960s. In an age of youthful rebellion, if Dylan did not actually say what the young thought, he at least articulated views that many wished they held. In any event, Dylan's evolving world view during the 1960s tells us much about the proverbial generation gap, while explaining why Dylan became a powerful cultural hero.[10]

Bob Dylan was not particularly typical of his age. More precisely he was typical of its alienation. He rejected the materialism of postwar America and sought spiritual fulfillment and artistic excellence instead. While neglecting the search for solutions, Dylan was nevertheless on the make for meaning. Thousands would walk that intellectual path in the late 1960s, but early in the decade Dylan was a relative pioneer—a drifter on the national cultural road. It is important to see Dylan throughout his career in a broad social context. His particular talent was the ability to react creatively to both events and the general climate of opinion. Later in his career the songs came increasingly from his own experiences, but earlier his lyrics traced the national experience. Fully to understand Dylan's impact, it is necessary to analyze the direction of his music even more closely than the course of his life.

Dylan's first three albums had steadily become more topical. The first, *Bob Dylan,* in 1962 had been completely folk-oriented—split between traditional ballads and his own personal songs. The second album, *The Freewheelin' Bob Dylan,* in 1963, was split between protest and folk ballads and included five antiwar and pro-civil rights songs, headed by "Blowin' in the Wind." His 1964 album, *The Times They Are A-Changin',* clearly typed him as a protest singer, since seven of the album's ten songs dealt with protest themes.

Thus in 1964 Dylan had come together with the age. He was logically hailed as the king of protest music. Though his appearance was scruffy his politics made him acceptable to most liberals. A 1964 *Harper's* article described him as "a cross between a beatnik and choir boy."[11] In April 1964 a *Life* article depicted Dylan as "The Angry Young Folk Singer" and a one-man truth squad. Bob was quoted as follows:

> The teachers in school taught me everything was fine.. . .But it ain't fine man.. . . Kids have a feeling like me, but they ain't hearin' it no place. They're scared to step out. But I ain't scared to do it man.[12]

Shortly thereafter Ralph Gleason, a respected popular music critic, hailed Dylan as "a genius, a singing conscience and moral referee as well as a preacher." For Gleason, Bob was a writer whose "poetic images" clearly posed "the moral dilemmas" of America and more importantly a man "made wise by a poetic vision of truth."[13] Perhaps Gleason got carried away with his rhetoric, but Dylan's protest songs did range the full spectrum of reform and usually set a standard in each area. For example, as "Blowin' in the Wind" became the chief Northern civil rights song, "Masters of War" became the standard pacifist ballad, while "A Hard Rain's A-Gonna Fall" served as the anthem of ban-the-bomb groups. Dylan's songs were featured in protest-song periodicals like *Broadside* and *Sing Out!* and he even became a blacklisted martyr when he refused to appear on the Ed Sullivan Show over the issue of censorship. In 1964 writer Richard Fariña, who had followed Dylan's career closely, summed up Bob's function by asserting that Dylan felt that it was "up to him to speak out for the millions around him who lack the fortitude to speak for themselves."

Then suddenly, with little warning, it was all over. Dylan the selfless reformer, the heir to Woody Guthrie, and the inspiration of a new generation of topical singers, slipped back into an intensely personal world and turned his back on social reform. Looking back now, it is apparent that Dylan never was a committed reformer, and that protest songs were only an accidental or perhaps inevitable stage of his music. However, at the time, Dylan had been overtaken by his legend. One cannot understand the hostility toward Dylan unless one understands the legend. The fact that Bob outrode the storm testifies to both his talent and charisma. Eventually Dylan would create new fans and win back old ones, but his protest image remained. Critics and older fans continued to stir the ashes of his pseudo-proletarian past awaiting the time Bob would return to his roots and lead the next great protest song revival. Yet, however false, Dylan's perennial messiah image was essential to his status as a cultural hero.

Over the short term, criticism of the new Dylan was intense. While a few of his older admirers praised his honesty, growth, and innovativeness, most charged him with selling out commercially. The opening salvo came in November 1964 with an open letter to Dylan from folk music critic Irwin Silber in *Sing Out!*. Silber suggested that fame was getting in Bob's way and that his new songs seemed to be all "inner-directed . . . inner-probing, self-conscious" and "maybe even a little maudlin." Silber accused Dylan of "relating to a handful of cronies behind the scenes" rather than the audience. While Silber acknowledged that Dylan need not be a writer of protest songs, he argued that any writer who tried to deal honestly with the real world was "bound to write protest songs." In conclusion Silber depicted Dylan as just another casualty of American-style capitalist success. According to Silber, in America:

> Unable to produce real art on its own, the Establishment breeds creativity in protest against and nonconformity to the System. And then through notoriety, fast money, and status, it makes it almost impossible for the artist to function and grow.[14]

The next month Dylan was more forcefully, if less artfully, castigated from the pages of *Broadside*. In an article titled "The New Dylan," songwriter-critic Paul Wolfe compared Bob with Phil Ochs. Needless to say, Dylan came in a rather poor second. Wolfe noted that at the recent Newport Folk Festival while Ochs told the government "I Ain't Marching Anymore," Dylan told "his perennial, anonymous girl friend," "All I really want to do is, baby, be friends with you."

For Wolfe the distinctions between Ochs and the new Dylan were "manifest: meaning versus innocuousness, sincerity versus utter disregard for the tastes of the audience, idealistic principle versus self-conscious egotism."[15]

Others were more tolerant, if somewhat disappointed. By far the best analysis of Dylan during this period was a *New Yorker* profile by Nat Hentoff which appeared in October 1964. Dylan told Hentoff that his newest album would not contain "any finger-pointing songs." Bob said that he would stand behind the protest songs he had written, but explained that some of the rationale for those earlier songs had been to get "into the scene, to be heard, and a lot of it was because" he had not seen anybody else writing those songs, Now that many singers were turning out protest music, Dylan no longer wanted to be "a spokesman," no longer wanted to "write for people."[16] Hentoff pressed about Bob's background and Dylan replied, "My background's not all that important though, it's what I am now that counts." Dylan explained his move away from "finger-pointing songs" by noting:

> I looked around and saw all these people pointing fingers at the bomb. But the bomb is getting boring, because what's wrong goes much deeper than the bomb. What's wrong is how few people are free. Most people walking around are tied down to something that doesn't let them really speak, so they just add their confusion to the mess. I mean, they have some kind of vested interest in the way things are now. Me, I'm cool.

Being cool meant being free. Asked why he kept running away from home and parents, Dylan replied, "because I wasn't free." Bob felt that even as a child he "knew that parents do what they do because they're up tight. They're concerned with their kids in relation to themselves. I mean, they want their kids to please them, not to embarrass them—so they can be proud of them." Dylan felt that everybody had to find his own mode of freedom, and if there was one theme running through his songs after 1964, it was personal freedom.[17]

Not surprisingly, when the subject turned to Dylan's break with the organized civil rights groups he had worked with before, the issue was reduced to personal freedom. Dylan said that while he had known black "Freedom Fighters" like Jim Forman (of SNCC) as individuals, the white Northern civil rights groups like the one that had given him their Tom Paine award were actually getting him to look at black people as black people. As for the individuals in the civil rights groups, Dylan suggested:

> They're doing their time. They're chained to everybody else. They're chained to what they're doing. The only thing is, they're trying to put morals and great deeds on their chains, but basically they don't want to jeopardize their positions. They got their jobs to keep.[18]

Bob now felt that although people constantly talked about changing society, as long as their major concern was protecting their status and possessions, little would be accomplished.

Something more basic had changed than Dylan's withdrawal from organized reform. Bob had long since taken off his Woody Guthrie mask. He was wealthy; he traveled first class, wore mod clothing, and toured Europe. He was through with physical hard traveling; his journeys would all be inward now. He would be moving away from groups—especially the working classes who were Guthrie's chosen people. Dylan had now come to fear the American masses. For most of Bob's old fans, it was a choice between politics and art. However, since Dylan had no politics, he never had to make a choice. Those who continued to praise Dylan did so in the name of art, since they were captured by his musical boldness. In 1965 Dylan had again made the top-forty record list with his own rendition of "Like A Rolling Stone." Moreover, his appearance and manner began to set a pattern for other cult heroes. Bob's hair, sometimes referred to as a "Jewish 'Fro," had grown so shaggy that he made the Beatles look clean-cut by comparison. Meanwhile, his approach to reporters and interviewers, while never friendly, had grown increasingly surly and unresponsive. Here and there Dylan stopped putting on reporters long enough to comment on his new music. In one 1965 interview he explained his move into electric music:

> I became interested in folk music because I had to make it
> somehow. Obviously I'm not a hard-working cat. I played the
> guitar, that was all I did. I thought it was great music. . . . I
> was doing fine, you know, singing and playing my guitar. It
> was a sure thing, don't you understand . . . I was getting very
> bored with that. I couldn't go out and play like that. I was
> thinking of quitting.[19]

Dylan was into drugs by 1965, and it was clear that he
was bored with both life and his older style music. Yet the
folk purists continued to label him a simple, commercial
sellout. Israel Young, an old Village admirer, stated that Bob
had "become a pawn in his own game." Young argued that
whereas Dylan's earlier songs projected "life, vivacity, statement, and protest" the recent ones indicated a "bitterness and
loneliness" that left you "depressed and alone, instead of
wanting to join with others in life and song." Young further
charged that Dylan tailored his performances for commercial
gain, that he sang "with two voices, clear and unclear," that
he would sing songs in England that he would not use in
America because his English audience was two years behind
its American counterparts. In conclusion Young suggested
that Dylan would soon be popular enough and safe enough
to entertain the troops.[20]

Other old admirers were much more optimistic about
Bob's new music. Phil Ochs, for example, was a constant
champion during this period. Phil thought that with the two
1965 albums, *Bringing It All Back Home* and *Highway 61
Revisited,* Dylan had reached an artistic peak. Ochs felt
Dylan's new songs were like great paintings in that you kept
hearing and seeing different things in them each time you
listened. Phil depicted Dylan as a poet writing in the musical
idiom and communicating to a broad intellectual spectrum
of youth in a way that no conventional poet had ever done.
The exciting thing was that Dylan's audience approached
him in infinitely various ways. As Ochs put it, they "were all
listening for different things," and Dylan thus became "LSD
set to music."[21]

Joan Baez saw Dylan in a more personal and less artistic

way. Bob had steadily drawn away from her as he moved into more personal music. Dylan and Baez were often billed as the king and queen of folk protest during the period from 1963 to 1965, yet by 1965 Baez felt that she was becoming "the peace queen" and he the "rock-and-roll king." Looking back on this era in 1970, Joan stressed Dylan's general confusion, hostility, and especially his paranoid response to fame. She characterized most of his ambivalence as defense mechanisms designed to keep him aloof from the world, and she sensed an increasingly psychotic aspect of his nature.[22] No doubt, their split was inevitable for political reasons, personal differences aside. While she was getting more involved in issues and less involved in music through her founding of the Institute for the Study of Nonviolence, Dylan was moving in the opposite direction. Nevertheless, Joan showed the mixture of awe, revulsion, and excitement common to those around Dylan in the 1965 era. In her autobiographical memoir, *Daybreak*, Joan labeled Bob the "Dada king," and illustrated her impassioned reaction by describing him in concert during 1965.

> He was a huge transparent bubble of ego. And I said yes to the sounds of his rage and his band and I listened and heard the words, the pleadings, the nonsense, the denials, and I almost drowned in it but came up over and over to call for more . . .[23]

Before the controversy over Dylan's new music had begun, he had indicated his new path in a January 1964 prose-poem letter to *Broadside*. It contained Bob's clearest statement on his role as a celebrity artist, though the letter, like his songs, was very loose and idiomatic. Dylan started by explaining his new fame:

> I am now famous . . . it snuck up on me and pulverized me . . . it is hard for me to walk down the same streets. . . . I don't know if I like givin my autograph, o yes sometimes I do . . . but other times the back of my mind tells me it is not honest . . . for I am just fulfillin a myth to somebody who'd actually treasure my handwritin more'n his handwritin . . . this gets very complicated for me an proves to me that I am living in a contradiction . . . to quote mr. froyd I get quite paranoyd . . .

The folksy Guthrie-like style, complete with misspellings, was an obvious attempt to show his old fans that although he was changing his music and had become famous he was still Woody's and *Broadside*'s boy. Yet Dylan tactfully indicated that he would no longer appeal for mass solutions, but would seek personal truth and express it, thus refusing to go against his conscience or his "own natural senses." Bob concluded:

> . . . for I think that that is all the truth there is . . . and no more thru all the gossip, lies, religions, cults, myths, gods, history books, social books, all books, politics, decrees, rules, laws, boundary lines, bibles, legends, and bathroom writings, there is no guidance at all except from ones own natural senses from being born an it can't be preached nor sold nor even understood . . .[25]

Dylan indirectly indicated that he still respected the *Broadside*, protest-song approach (by praising Phil Ochs and Pete Seeger), but he insisted that this had never been his personal style. At one point he asked: "An what am I anyway? Some kind of messiah walking around . . .?[26] The letter was a good example of Dylan's prose, despite its hastiness. The words projected mood as well as content, style as well as substance, humor as well as seriousness, questions as well as answers, and warmth as well as aloofness.

While Dylan's move away from protest had surprised many people, his recent past provided consistent evidence that he was on his own trip and hardly harnessed to a movement. The times had changed markedly from 1964 to 1966, but Dylan had changed even faster. His album covers during this period tell the story. On *The Times They Are A-Changin'* album in 1964, Bob appeared in stark black and white, dressed in workshirt and dungarees, with a classic proletarian facial expression—a vision of hope and patience. On the next three album covers, from *Another Side of Bob Dylan* in 1965 to *Blonde on Blonde* in 1966, Dylan made a steady transformation from road-weary friend of the masses to ascetic guru of the hip. His hair grew wilder, his expression more distant, his clothes more outlandish, the scenes became more improbable, and on *Blonde on Blonde* the entire album cover was blurred. Dylan, always older than his years, began to feel older while his songs proclaimed that he was thinking younger. In 1965 he told a newspaper reporter, "I'm not a voice of their generation. How can I be? I'm not of their generation."[27]

In his rare interviews Dylan gave coded answers about his world view. Back in 1963 he had told *Newsweek,* "I am my words." However one could always understand his songs better than his comments. Periodically, Dylan probably said more than he meant to. For example, when a Chicago reporter suggested that Bob was "terribly separated from people," Dylan replied:

> I'm not disconnected from anything because of a force, just habit, it's just the way I am . . . I have an idea, that it's easier to be disconnected than to be connected. . . . I've been connected so many times. Things haven't worked out right, so rather than break myself up, I just don't get connected . . .
>
> Some day I might find myself all alone in a subway car, stranded when the lights go out, with 40 people, and I'll have to get to know them. Then I'll just do what has to be.[28]

His interview with *Playboy*'s Nat Hentoff in 1966 was a good example of Bob's usual press patter—eighty per cent abstract put-on and the rest subtle jibes at the liberal establishment. When Hentoff asked if he had "any unfulfilled ambitions," Bob replied that he had "always wanted to be Anthony Quinn in *La Strada*" and also always yearned "to be Brigitte Bardot." As to whether he had the "standard boyhood dream" of becoming President, Dylan answered: "No. When I was a boy, Harry Truman was President; who'd want to be Harry Truman?" Only when Hentoff inquired about protest music or Bob's earlier background did he get a semiserious answer. Asked whether he "had any regrets about not completing college," Dylan suggested that colleges were "like old-age homes," except that many more people died in colleges than in homes for the elderly. When asked if he would like to help youths grow up to be different from their parents, Dylan answered that he did not know their parents. Bob observed that he was "really not the right person to tramp around the country saving souls." Suddenly turning very serious, Dylan concluded:

I wouldn't run over anybody that was laying in the street, and I certainly wouldn't become a hangman. I wouldn't think twice about giving a starving man a cigarette. But I'm not a shepherd. And I'm not about to save anybody from a fate, which I know nothing about. . . . The key word is "destiny." I can't save them from that.[29]

Late in July 1966 Jules Siegel's feature article on Dylan appeared in the *Saturday Evening Post.* Siegel had interviewed Dylan and pictured Bob as the soul of popular music—a man at the very peak of his career and influence, an artist "who at 25 admits he's a millionaire but denies being a genius." Ironically, Dylan's severe motorcycle accident occurred the same week the article came out. After the accident Dylan took a long time to appear in person and even longer to demonstrate his new artistic mood. In his first post-recovery interview in May 1967, the reporter found Dylan wary and thin, but relatively tranquil. In Bob's most philosophical interview comment, he observed: "A man is a success if he gets up in the mornin' and gets to bed at night and in between he does what he wants to. What I want to do is make music."[30]

The new music materialized in his *John Wesley Harding* album, released in January 1968. It was, without doubt, Dylan's biggest musical change since he dropped protest songs. The new album had the major Dylan trademark— word imagery—but it was generally more subdued. There has already been a tremendous escalation in imagery, from his earlier topical songs to the psychedelic cuts on his last two albums, *Highway 61 Revisited* and *Blonde on Blonde.* Talking about peace and justice "blowin' in the wind" was one thing, but a "motorcycle black madonna two-wheeled gypsy queen" was quite another. Dylan was now back to more low-key phrases. Yet the new songs had a universality that defied interpretation. Several critics suggested that Dylan was going back to his earlier style. Bob did make extensive use of acoustical guitar and harmonica on *Harding,* but now the musical style was just a backdrop for the song lyrics. Dylan had always been a musical innovator, but here the change was more verbal and philosophical. The sober lyrics of somber-sounding songs like "I Dreamed I Saw St. Augustine" and "I Pity the Poor Immigrant" transcended the personal vision of Bob's recent songs and projected a more cosmic outlook. If his older songs had captured the times and his recent songs had reflected his experiences, the new songs suggested Dylan's views on the most fundamental questions about life. No doubt the prime factor was his accident and close brush with death. Whereas the earlier songs were directly connected to particular times, places, and events, the *John Wesley Harding* songs existed in a cultural vacuum. Dylan now sang about a "poor immigrant" who "passionately" hated "his life," yet "likewise" feared "his death."[31] Bob explained that the moral of "The Ballad of Frankie Lee and Judas Priest" was that when you found a "neighbor carryin' something," you should "help him with his load" and not mistake "paradise" for some "home across the road." In "The Wicked Messenger" Dylan told the messenger that if he could not "bring good news," then not to "bring any." Somewhat prematurely, writer Al Aronowitz concluded that "at age 26 Dylan" was back and he was "pulling out the electric plug."[32]

The new lyrics were less abstract. Ironically that made them more difficult to understand, since most critics had long since given up trying to find specific meanings in Dylan's songs and had concentrated on mood instead. The field for Dylan interpretation was now wide open again. Alan Weberman, a self-proclaimed "Dylanologist" who had continued to decipher Bob's songs, had a head start on later arrivals. Weberman had a field day with *John Wesley Harding*. He maintained that Dylan's new songs were subtle, coded protest songs about everything in contemporary America from the Vietnam war to the greediness of the music industry.[33] Since the words lent themselves to unlimited interpretation, there was no way Weberman could be proven wrong. Gordon Friesen, editor of *Broadside,* was anxious to believe that Dylan was returning to protest and ambitious enough to try to analyze Bob's new song, "The Mighty Quinn," in terms of Vietnam. Friesen suggested the following meanings for the first verse:

> "Everybody's building ships and boats"—to get men and guns to Vietnam. "Some are building monuments"—gravestones for the dead. Others jotting down notes"—piling up banknotes, profits from the war. But "Everybody's in despair"—everyone in America knows that in spite of all the sacrifices and effort the war is going to be lost.[34]

On balance, Friesen's explanation seemed as valid as Weberman's, which went to show that Dylan continued to be what you wanted him to be. Joan Baez was stricken with the same fevered hopefulness about a new Dylan. She recorded a double-album of Dylan songs, including several from *John Wesley Harding*.

Looking back from the vantage point of 1970, Steven Goldberg, an academic Dylanologist, saw Dylan as a mystic. Bob's art, according to Goldberg, was "the poetry of salvation," and his achievement was being able to communicate the primary mystic insight: "All distinction is illusory." Goldberg found it logical for Dylan to be popular at a time of crisis, for only then were people dissatisfied enough to search for the mystical. He felt that Dylan's "conception of a transcendence that flows through man" steadily shaded into compassion and reached a stage of completion with *John Wesley Harding*, which Goldberg considered Dylan's "supreme work"[35]

Jon Landau, editor of *Rolling Stone*, had a rather restrained review of *John Wesley Harding*. Analyzing the album in general terms only, he found it to be Dylan's declaration of independence from the current musical styles. He also saw its American folk themes as a pointed message to Beatle fans that he was an American artist. Landau disclaimed knowledge of any specific messages in the ballads, yet he argued that the new Dylan songs acknowledged the Vietnam war in the same way that such Beatle songs as "Magical Mystery Tour" and "Fool on the Hill" ignored it. On balance, he found the new Dylan to be "profoundly moral" without being specifically moralistic.[36] Perhaps Paul Williams, editor of the music magazine, *Crawdaddy,* had the safest approach to the new Dylan. Williams observed that if *John Wesley Harding* was "unfathomable, at least the soundings are good." Williams was not worried about understanding Dylan. According to him there was "no freedom involved in understanding," because whenever you understood something

> you've gone and done it even if you chose not to. And since you and I never quite see through the same eyeballs anyway, what do you care who understands which? We'll all grow old together.[37]

Dylan's next record, *Nashville Skyline,* released in April 1969, took most reviewers and fans by surprise. On the album cover was a smiling Bob Dylan tipping his hat. On the record were a number of happy, sometimes syrupy country-and-western style songs celebrating life and love. In a *Rolling Stone* review, Paul Nelson, who had found *John Wesley Harding,* "not unlkike Jean-Paul Sartre playing the five-string banjo," found *Nashville Skyline* "a deep, humane, and interesting statement about being happy."[38] However Nelson was a long-time Dylanophile. Many Dylan fans were disappointed by the simplicity of the new songs. They expected profundity and instead got a duet with Johnny Cash on one cut. Yet almost everybody agreed that the album was musically superb and that Dylan's voice here showed a new softness, range, and versatility. Moreover, one album cut, "Lay Lady Lay," a sexy and sexist song, captured the teen market and became a top-ten single. To add insult to injury (for those celebrating Dylan's supposed return to seriousness), in June 1970 Dylan released *Self Portrait,* a dual album of old standards like "Blue Moon." Once again the cries of commercial sell-out appeared. Even Dylan's most faithful supporters in the rock press found it hard to praise *Self Portrait.* For most critics, Dylan singing other people's songs was like Robert Frost reciting the poems of Edgar Guest or Rod McKuen.

Yet in November 1970, before the howling had reached

its peak, Dylan released *New Morning,* a new album of his own songs. The record drew almost universal acceptance and praise for its combination of imaginative and provocative lyrics with heavier rock arrangments than had been used on the past three albums. Ed Ward's *Rolling Stone* review began: "Well, friends, Bob Dylan is back again. I don't know how long he intends to stay, but I didn't ask him. Didn't figure it was any of my business."[39] Ralph Gleason, another *Rolling Stone* contributor, titled a story, "We've Got Dylan Back Again." Once again, as after the 1967 accident, Dylan was reborn. And when late in 1971, Dylan brought out a single record, "George Jackson," a memorial to the "Soledad Brother" slain in an attempted prison break, it appeared that Dylan was moving back to protest songs. Indeed, the song was one of the few specific topical songs ever to make the top-forty charts. Naturally enough *Broadside* was delirious with joy. The November 1971 issue printed the lyrics of "George Jackson" on the front page and underneath was the headline "Welcome Back, Bob." *Broadside* editor Gordon Friesen explained that with this new song Dylan had returned to, and politically surpassed, "the great topical song-writing of his early years." Friesen agreed with Alan Weberman that "George Jackson" rose above Dylan's earlier songs, for here Bob placed "himself squarely beside a truly heavy revolutionary, calling" Jackson "a man I really loved."[40] Although the song's message created little public stir, Dylan's use of the line, "he wouldn't take shit from no one," caused the song to be banned by numerous stations until the offending word was bleeped out. As usual, the *Broadside* rejoicing was premature. Dylan evidently wrote the song on impulse after reading *Soledad Brother: The Prison Letters of George Jackson.* Bob did not follow up with additional topical ballads and did not even release a new album until late in 1973, just before he embarked on a nostalgic but ambitious concert tour with The Band. The 1973 album, *Planet Waves,* was a throwback to *Nashville Skyline* with songs that registered love and contentment. Nevertheless, Dylan's new record and concert tour set off the usual excitement and hopes. In

January 1974 there was Bob staring at us from the cover of *Newsweek* with the now familiar headline, "Dylan's Back."

In yet another way Bob Dylan disappointed the faithful. In May 1971 his long-awaited novel, *Tarantula,* was published. The book, largely written between 1964 and 1966, was released when Bob was turning out little else. It proved what many had long known, that Dylan is not a particularly clever prose writer. The book reads like one long, abstract record liner note.[41] Forced to rely on words alone, Dylan the writer gets panicky and throws in too much description and not enough craft. The images are too bulky, the wit too forced, and the pace too fast. The magic musical style and timing that could hold his most abstract songs together are not possible in a book. *Tarantula* underscored an important truth. Dylan's power was always in his music; the words were important, but always secondary to the music. Bob's magic was aural and cultural. Taken out of its peculiar element it could not survive. Dylan's success with the young directly supports Marshall McLuhan's media theories. McLuhan argues that the aural sense is beginning to dominate our society again. He asserts that the younger generation have an older tribal sensory balance which is both more aural and tactile, and that they learn more by participating in pattern recognition than by observing the printed word. The problem, contends McLuhan, is that most teachers are visual, literate, and print-minded and thus tend to compartmentalize learning, both by subject and method. Whatever else can be said about Dylan's music, it certainly rates high in its ability to merge subject matter and induce tactile response from listeners. Clearly, Dylan is not a traditional poet. Some feel he is not a poet at all, yet few would deny the magic of his songs. However, Dylan is not a consistent prose sorcerer. Mixed in with the magic phrases are large numbers of "missed" metaphors, middle-class clichés, and grammar school rhymes. In some songs, he insists that one good image deserves a dozen others. Few serious poets would have the gall to turn a Woody Guthrie-style phrase like "You insane tongues of war talk/Ain't a-gonna guide my road,"[42] on the one hand and later, in a supposed maturity, indulge in the sophomoric line, "And the National Bank at a profit sells road maps for the soul."[43]

"I am my words," Dylan asserted in 1963, and finally Dylan must be understood in terms of his lyric ballads. Pete Seeger has pointed out that Dylan was "essentially a writer, not a performer." Seeger felt that when a writer created something, he was finished and restlessly moved on to something else. The performer, however, recreated a song "and through many performances" explored "the subtle changes of meaning" that he sensed "in different times and places."[44] Too often, Dylan created a storm by his performance, either his change to electric rock, or his psychedelic clothes, or incoherent verbiage to reporters. What difference that Bob gave up the simple folksinger style to rock-and-roll like a single, mindless Beatle? What matter that he gave up jeans for tasteless mod combinations of clothes? What significance in his continual hostility to the press? Dylan was a highstrung artist and since the gifted are often eccentric, his appearance and actions should have gained wider tolerance. However, many of his fans and the general public approached him as a performer. The problem was that Dylan had earlier conned many into believing that he was either a simple lovable drifter or a liberal political activist. Yet despite his earlier mannerisms his lyrics always gave him away. From first to last he was an alienated artist, who self-consciously stood apart from society.

Dylan had a classic existential focus, long before he understood existentialism as a philosophy. Bob sensed the absurd aspects of society as an isolated teenager, and as a young adult he concluded that idealism too was absurd. What remained was his desire to find the truth that he alone could perceive. To seek wider meanings was both pointless and useless. Thus, Dylan's critique of society was truly beyond left and right. His songs were a nonideological fortress from which to launch attacks on social myths. His weapons were images of a decadent society filtered through his one angle of vision. Bob's songs were often more effective than the rational warnings of radicals because they spoke in youth's idiom and projected mood rather than argument. Arguments could be met with counter-arguments, but Dylan's songs slipped into your consciousness unaware. Suddenly it was not a matter of what you thought, but of what you felt. After listening to several post–1965 Dylan songs, you were not surprised about the Vietnam war or urban neighborhoods burning to the ground. Bob's powerful, surreal images and the world's absurdity complemented each other perfectly. The songs told us indirectly what everyone began to feel—that society no longer worked; and the proof was that social ideals could not be passed on to the young. The older ideals were material ones, and whereas Dylan felt that his father never "transcended the pain of material things," Bob felt that he had, since he would do what he did whether he "was paid for it or not."[45] The problem for Dylan's older fans was that Bob's existential escape was necessarily personal and thus, in their eyes, self-indulgent. They were uninterested in personal visions. They wanted songs to stir the masses with visions of either social shame or political solutions. Yet even the old Dylan never sang for the proletarian masses; his audiences had always been the literate middle classes. He made the reformers feel better, not the oppressed.

Dylan amassed his own personal army, though he never acknowledged them. His folk-protest fans had admired his skill, but his most fervent admirers were those teenagers who after 1965 saw him as the champion of their side of the generation gap. The kids may not have understood all of Bob's lyrics, but they were confident that their parents understood nothing about the songs. Yet Dylan was always too intellectual to be the voice of teenage America. He served instead as their adult guru—a status symbol who proved that rock was both serious and articulate. Dylan's range was much wider than that of most popular rock artists. His fans covered the spectrum from young to old, rich to poor, and right to left. And if Dylan was difficult to fully comprehend, unlike most intellectuals he was at least exciting and pleasurable to listen to. More importantly, he took poetic songs out of esoteric coffeehouses and small specialized concerts and put them on the public airwaves. The radio carried his nightmarish, existential messages to the young, unwashed, and culturally deprived—people who were usually beyond the reach of social reformers. Evidently, Bob was proud of his range, if somewhat reluctant to draw conclusions about its results. In a 1966 interview Dylan was asked why he thought music was "more in tune with what was happening." With uncharacteristic fervor, he replied:

> Great paintings shouldn't be in museums. Have you ever been in a museum? Museums are cemeteries. Paintings should be on the walls of restaurants, in dimestores, in gas stations, in men's rooms. Great paintings should be where people hang out. The only thing where it's happening is on the radio and records, that's where people hang out.[46]

The strength of Dylan's music was that it reflected what was happening without either pandering to any one social group or suggesting what should be happening. The old-time protesters argued that this amoral position rejected personal social responsibility and encouraged the young to adopt a nihilistic world view. However, Dylan was no more a hippie for having given up direct protest. The flower children tried to escape society and make a world of their own; Dylan was always trying to make some sense of the larger society. Bob reflected the hippie sensibility, but was never its advocate. Dylan especially caught the imagination of college students, although he was a college dropout who equated higher education with intellectual babysitting and general immaturity. Similarly, Bob was often venerated by leftist activists, even though he clearly put down direct political action. Yet Dylan vividly reflected the student left's contempt for middle-class American liberals. Dylan had a genius for feeling and reflecting things without being caught up in them. In addition, once Dylan's reputation as a perceptive mirror of the times was established, he became a self-fulfilling prophecy. His existential personal lyrics allowed everybody to interpret his phrases as a coded comment on what they perceived to be *the* crucial social trend. Dylan increasingly became all things to all people, although he generally was much closer to the radical "New Left" than to their liberal competition. The liberals too saw the gap between American ideals and social reality and sought to close it. However, Dylan's songs cast doubt on American ideals themselves. Thus they offered support to those who rejected traditional reform in favor of the activist's radical political change or the dropout's total rejection. Clearly Dylan felt himself in opposition; he was always a nay-sayer rather than a yea-sayer. Bob was always most appealing to his fans in the act of rejection. In his early career his songs generally rejected racism or warmongering. Later the ballads often rejected individuals, usually women, but sometimes unnamed male acquaintances as well. Finally, Bob rejected his earlier self (the protest singer) and turned to songs that rejected society at large. As a man who projected a consistent alienated image, he remained a fitting cultural hero for an age of alienation.

Dylan is presently uninterested in analyzing or talking about his past music and life. The last two extensive interviews he gave were with *Sing Out!* in 1968 and with *Rolling Stone* in 1969. The *Sing Out!* interview once more centered on his move away from protest songs. On this point Dylan depicted himself as changing with the times and by implication suggested that his old fans were static. Bob felt it was easy to write a protest song back then since "there were thousands and thousands of people just wanting that song." However, he felt that he no longer had "the capacity to feed" the force that needed "all these songs." And when asked why his songs were not "as socially or politically applicable as they were earlier," Dylan replied, "Probably that is because no one cares to see it the way I'm seeing it now, whereas before, I saw it the way they saw it."[47] The *Rolling Stone* interview was Dylan's last extended public comment. He noted that although he generally avoided interviews and press conferences because the media used him to sell papers, he had consented to this interview because it was with a "music paper." Dylan was as self-consciously hip, world-weary, and cynical as ever, but most of his hostility had disappeared; he seemed more confident and more at peace. On the old question of whether Dylan was a "youth leader," he replied that if he was he "would be out there doing it" like "the Maharishi." Bob noted that instead he was only playing music, writing songs, and "staying out of people's hair." On the relationship between drugs and his older songs, Dylan indicated that his drug experiences had not affected the content of supposed drug songs like "Mr. Tambourine Man," but that drugs had kept him going physically so he could continue to "pump" the songs "out." When asked if he had voted for President in 1968, Bob laughingly replied that he had "got down to the polls too late." Dylan talked easily about music, but when the conversation strayed from musical style or tastes, he became distant, nonsensical, or just folks. Near the end he was asked whether he saw himself as "a poet, a singer, a rock-and-roll star, married man . . . " He answered: "All of those. I see myself as it all. . . . I'll be it all. I feel 'confined' when I have to choose one or the other."[48]

Yet, Dylan's avoidance of direct, rational comment for the press was always a shrewd tactic. Bob was never a particularly sophisticated or witty commentator on current events, even in the world of music, although he often displayed a wry, penetrating humor, oddly reminiscent of Woody Guthrie. And invariably his quite ordinary comments would be judged against his brilliant songwriting. Dylan could only dispel his mystique by playing it straight with reporters. Without doubt, the image has remained intact, for in his successful concert tour of 1974, the crowd generally came to venerate the legendary, mystic Dylan. Bob accommodated them by playing a good portion of his program with acoustic guitar and retaining his long-standing aloofness. "Dylan's back and it's still all right," crowed a *Chicago Sun-Times* headline after Bob's Chicago concert. *Newsweek* reported that when the "32-year-old Dylan" came onstage, he "was the Dylan everyone remembered: skinny, hunched over, dressed simply in blue jeans and black wool shirt."[49] The older fans had come for nostalgia, the younger ones to hear a new musical revelation for the 1970s and just to see their hero in the flesh. However, Bob could only offer nostalgia. He did sing some new songs, but they hardly pointed to a new musical era. Dylan was no longer rapidly changing, and it was unlikely that his music could change markedly. Bob's songs reflected his contentment and advanced age by providing maturer versions of his old messages. To replace his bitter 1965 farewell to protest in the song, "Back Pages," he now sang that it had never been his "duty to remake the world at large," nor was it his "intention to sound the battle charge." Instead he was going to concentrate on his love for his wife and children. He also sang a song titled, "Forever Young," which offered the hope that one might remain forever busy, forever happy, and forever young. The song underscored both Bob's problem and his triumph. Dylan was forever aging. In "Back Pages," he had sung that he was much older during his protest period, and was "younger than that now." However, by the 1970s he had given up youthful idealism for mature cynicism and age had overtaken him. He is viable today only because his reclusiveness and aloofness nourish his older mystique. He had grown older against his will. Dylan could outrun the adoring mobs of fans and escape the musical trends and fads, but finally he could not escape history. He would always be a part of the 1960s—a cultural hero frozen in time. In the soulless 1970s he was a symbol, not of the phony political and musical present, but of the rich, vibrant past. He could please an audience with still artful lyrics and increased musical mastery, but he had lost his magic ability to reflect the social mood.

Dylan was always a counter-cultural force. In the terms of Marxist criticism he was a writer who had worked against the ruling ideology by illustrating the contradictions endemic to the established system. Thus Dylan raised the consciousness of youth, even while refusing to urge revolution. However, Dylan's latest songs only point out ironies. His nightmarish visions of a society bent on reducing people to its materialistic common denominator are gone. Bob is suddenly at home in the world he never made. Buoyed up by his wealth, secure in the warmth of his immediate family, Dylan the drifter has found his permanent happy valley. Finally, Bob had become what he had always claimed to be, just a musician doing his thing. Now suddenly Dylan had it all together, but he had lost his peculiar artistic view, and with it the substance of his charisma. The cultural hero had turned into a musical celebrity.

CODA:
THE END OF AN ERA

8: The Day the Music Died

After 1968, protest music increasingly lost its meaning. It no longer sufficed to suggest that a song protested. One also had to inquire whether its protest lay primarily in its lyrics, music, style, or even in the performer's manner and dress. In short, did the song have an obvious message, or did it drive home its point in some subtle, symbolic, cultural code? Blatant message music had long since been driven to the cultural fringes by sophisticated ridicule and dwindling commercial success. It was no longer stylish or profitable to sing directly about social evils. Muckraking lyrics now often insulted an audience's intelligence. The young ears that strained to pick up the vibrations of protest music were usually already convinced that the nation was hung up, corrupt, and decaying. They wanted to know how to confront the situation or at least how to live with it.

At the same time, the new generation shrank from the syrupy phrase, the tired cliché, and the maudlin play on emotions. For example, those critics who caustically attacked the romantic emotionalism of Erich Segal's *Love Story* usually overlooked the generally unemotional, understated, low-keyed conversation of the novel's collegiate couple—especially Jenny's aversion to the Madison Avenue superlative. *Love Story*'s dialogue was typical of this generation's desire to complete conversational blanks mutely and make communication a veritable crossword puzzle. *Love Story* aptly illustrated an important new generational myth—the notion that people who really understood one another did so intuitively rather than verbally.

This tendency was easily observed in the contemporary, popular balladry—in the hazy lyrics of Bob Dylan, Paul Simon, and Joni Mitchell, for example, or the frenetic beat of the Rolling Stones or Jefferson Airplane. The words, style, and music were all open to various poetic interpretations. They were really do-it-yourself protest songs, since you could read your own problems into them and reap existential answers or solace in return. Another symptom of the breakdown of meaning lay in the relationships between the performer, the song, and the audience. One primary characteristic of the traditional folk-protest singer was an inclination to spend as much time introducing and explaining the song as singing it. If the contemporary singer spoke to the audience at all, he tended to talk about everything except the song.

Another striking development of contemporary protest music was the terminal illness overtaking various folk-protest orthodoxies. The arty attitude of the *Little Sandy Review*, which in 1962 could condemn a "Protesty song" as one that was "neither true protest nor true song," was necessarily suspect to a generation that identified "true" anything with rigid ideology or social brainwashing.[1] Meanwhile *Broadside*, the major butt of *Sandy Review*'s barbed wit, because of the former periodical's tendency to protest with every line of every topical song it published, had largely become a literary forum. The mostly mediocre topical ballads it printed became secondary to its often stimulating commentary on the musical scene and its usually sopho-moric social criticism. *Sing Out!* made a valiant attempt to bridge the gap between the ideological and artistic tradition-alists on the one hand and the loose, diverse counter-culture enthusiasts on the other, but the compromise did not satisfy many. Probably *Rolling Stone,* the psychedelic newspaper, more accurately reflected the vague amorphous nature of contemporary protest music. Amid this cultural chaos, it was not surprising that in 1970 Irwin Silber, former editor of *Sing Out!* and leader of protest song movements since 1945, concluded that "the once vital folk song movement in America" was "either hopelessly co-opted by the marketplace or reduced to the level of a white, middle-class suburban hobby."[2]

Somewhere along the way folk-protest was swallowed by the general musical category called rock. Musically, rock had assimilated the whole of American music, from rag-time to gospel, and thus folk-protest was hardly the only genre to be devoured whole. Yet there was something especially sad in its gradual and practically unnoticed demise. Here and there, record stores began filing folk-protest albums in with those of the rock super stars. There was surely no other place for a Bob Dylan, but it somehow seemed sacrilegious to find Joan Baez albums stacked in front of those of the theatrical transvestite David Bowie, or to see Phil Ochs albums sand-wiched between Procul Harum records and those of Nico and the Velvet Underground.

Folk-protest had its commercial side, but it also had a proud heritage and left an important social legacy. Rock, however, consumed all and left nothing but the music. From folk-rock to acid-rock to country-rock, the music moved on, but in no particular direction. From single performers to small groups to super bands and back again, the rock musicians moved around, but not toward anything. Rock reflected a great deal about the people who created and supported it, but it lacked any tangible reason for being, beyond commercial success. Some rock groups supposedly existed for grander purposes. The MC5 (a Detroit group), for example, styled themselves as "musical guerrillas," and flaunted their White Panther Party membership cards. Similarly, in 1968 Grace Slick, lead singer of the Jefferson Airplane, had performed their hit song, "Crown of Creation" in blackface and ended the number with the Black Panther salute. Not to be outdone, the MC5 borrowed two onstage stunts from The Fugs, an earlier hard rock group, and began taking off their clothes and burning the American flag during concert performances. Yet the entire rock-revolutionary trend quickly became indistinguishable from the self-conscious publicity-seeking known as "hype." It mattered little whether you burned your guitar or the flag, or whether, like male rock star Alice Cooper, you were content with chopping the head off a baby doll. The end result was meaningless theatrics. Rock concerts provided musical performances to see and hear, but hardly to think about, and many rock fans quickly lost interest in performers who just stood there and sang. Thus the strength of folk music—strong solid lyrics—has largely been the weakness of rock. There have been dozens of recent rock groups able to turn out tremendous melodic rock, but unable to match their instrumental virtuosity to a meaningful song. Lyrics depend on thought, and rock has largely been feeling. A number of young song writers, from Joni Mitchell to Leonard Cohen to Cat Stevens, have consistently turned out beautiful, artful songs. Nevertheless, no matter how haunting or spellbinding, the songs existed in a musical vacuum. For the age of rock is only a musical bazaar, increasingly filled with what the industry calls "product." "You pays your money and you takes your choice," in the American vernacular. Only the oil crisis and the consequent higher cost of vinyl discs seemed able to limit that choice. Indeed, it was this something-for-everybody attitude which first produced folk-rock.

That folk-rock increasingly meant all things to all people was ironically illustrated by equally vigorous attacks on the new music from both the right and the left. Such fiercely fundamentalist and anticommunist groups as the Tulsa-based Christian Crusade attacked folk-rock as a Marx-

ist plot to subvert the nation's youth. This view was particularly explicit in such Crusade publications as Reverend
David Noebel's book, *Rhythm, Riots, and Revolution* and
his pamphlet, *Columbia Records: Home of Marxist Minstrels.* However, Irwin Silber, a Marxist-oriented cultural
critic, and one of Noebel's major villains, recently concluded
that popular music threatened radical reform. Silber argued
that "groovy life styles" induced the masses to ignore the
system that oppressed them rather than to struggle to change
it.[3] No doubt, the anticommunist Christian fundamentalists
now feared electronic music less as a vanguard of atheistic
Marxism and more as an emotional substitute for religious
fundamentalism. Both fundamentalism and psychedelic
music had a sensory stress that appealed to emotion over
reason and the heart as opposed to the intellect.

After 1968 there suddenly seemed little or nothing to
revere. Such still-popular topical singers as Tom Paxton,
Joan Baez, and Phil Ochs still considered themselves to be
"Woody's Children," but the young audiences who listened
to their slickly arranged, orchestrated ballads usually found
Woody Guthrie's songs corny, simplistic, and irrelevant.
Pete Seeger could still occasionally spring his sing-along
charisma at an antiwar or antipollution rally, but on television and records the youth generally found him quaint and
dull. It was fitting and logical that songs sung in the simple,
unvarnished Guthrie-Seeger style were most often country-
and-western topical ballads that appealed to the prejudices of
an older, middle-America—songs like "Please Mr. Professor,"
"Welfare Cadillac," and "Okie from Muskogee."[4] These new
protest songs on the right were destroying another folk-
protest myth—specifically, the legend that topical songs
appealing to the discontented common "folk" were almost
by definition ballads sympathetic to social reform.

Increasingly, the classic protest song tradition lived not
in the folk, but in the memory and articles of academicians
and folklorists who continued to inquire about the roots,
ideology, and continuity of the folk revival. Of course, one
could do away with distasteful arguments about cultural

continuity by adopting Bob Dylan's conclusion that "it's all just music." Yet this hardly satisfied those intellectual scholars commonly described as compulsive generalizers, nor did it calm those remnants of the Guthrie-Seeger tradition who saw topical music as a lever for social reform.

That overt protest music had declined was universally acknowledged. There was less agreement about the reasons for its demise. The causes of collapse were literally legion. They ranged from the commercial to the creative to the psychological. Protest music declined because guru Bob Dylan continually refused to lead some new magical protest renaissance. It degenerated as it became clear that the poetic songs of Paul Simon and other writers were messageless patchwork ballads that reflected only the author's desire to create artful songs.[5] Protest music declined because the combination of social commitment and folk music was ridiculed by many alienated artists who felt that politics was sin and involvement was hopeless. Some writers and singers felt they were wasting their time preaching to an audience already on their side. For example, early in 1969, Judy Collins gave up singing protest songs because she no longer wanted to "be a political agitator" with her music, constantly facing an audience she recognized from the last rally. Suddenly Judy decided that protest songs were "like hitting people over the head" and "finger pointing"; and that the end result was "not a statement of emotional depth, but of unity in the face of an . . . enemy or idea which does not agree with" you. Moreover, she felt that protest music divided people when it should unite them. As Arlo Guthrie had noted, "You don't accomplish very much singing protest songs to people who agree with you. Everybody just has a good time thinking they're right."[6]

In 1970 Gordon Friesen, editor of *Broadside*, complained that although a number of good protest songs were being written, many folksingers sold out by singing "meaningless fluff about . . . clouds, flowers, butterflies . . . Suzannes . . . and the like"[7] Indeed, some former topical singers even avoided the term "folksinger" by describing themselves as singers of "contemporary art songs." Typical of these new folk-style art singers was Joni Mitchell, who in 1967 confessed that she felt "helpless" when she thought about Vietnam or Berkeley, since she had never been political and was still undecided about what she felt was "right for the world." She simply wrote about what happened to her. A similar case was Janis Ian, a precocious young folk star who at age thirteen had written "Society's Child," a perceptive protest song about race discrimination. Two years later, in 1968, she reported that she was concentrating on "mood songs." And Tim Hardin, the gifted author of "If I Were a Carpenter" and a composer with roots deep in the folk tradition, declared that he was "too involved" in his personal life "to write about the world." As singer Donovan Leitch put it in November 1969, the "best writers" had "evolved to the point" where they "left protest behind and beauty" crept in.[8] Perhaps a 1970 *New Yorker* cartoon summed up the new attitude best. It pictured a young female folksinger (guitar in hand) about to begin her performance at a coffeehouse. However, before commencing she advised her audience that since her songs had no "social or political significance" she would like to assure them that she was opposed to the Vietnamese war and in favor of legalizing marijuana, boycotting California grapes, and Federal control of the economy.[9]

Woody Guthrie had long been considered the root of the folk-protest movement and the younger singers like Baez and Dylan were considered the branches. Ironically, the flowers seemed to be singers like Joni Mitchell and Janis Ian, who had given up social involvement with little apparent remorse. Guthrie would no doubt have appreciated their musical talent, but presumably would not have rejoiced at their low social voltage. Yet there had been a time in the 1960s when folk-protest singers Dylan, Ochs, and Baez chilled the blood of conservative leaders and inspired the hearts of thousands who sought social change. The young protest singers had committed themselves to social action, and their songs were both calls to arms and indictments of the status quo. However, by the decade's end all but Baez had become disillusioned with musical agitation.

In 1967 topical singer Phil Ochs could fire up sophisticated radical activists. James Kunen, a radical Columbia student, attended an Ochs concert in Central Park and wrote in his diary: "After listening to Phil Ochs, I'm ready not only to burn City Hall, but to charge out and stuff envelopes or distribute leaflets or even sit at a meeting."[10] However, the same general frustrations that radicalized activist youth also drove protest writers like Ochs to despair and destroyed their creativity. Ochs's songs steadily became more revolutionary in spirit and more pessimistic about the future of American society. In a 1969 album, *Rehearsals for Retirement*, he sang an apocalyptic song titled, "A New Age," which aptly reflected his new mood. The ballad noted that considering the soldier's sorrow and the rage of the wretched, Americans should "pray for the aged," since we were approaching "the dawn of another age." The song later commented that while America was "born in a revolution," it "died in a wasted war." On the record jacket, Ochs bemoaned the fate of an America "imprisoned by" its "paranoia" and he concluded:

> My responsibilities are done, let them come, let them come.
> And I realize these last days these trials and tragedies were after all, only our rehearsals for retirement.[11]

Perhaps Theo Bikel was right back in 1967, when he asserted that "the protest song movement . . . had been shattered on the realities of American politics."[12] Moreover, as the despair of radicals mounted, it became harder to decide whether formerly activist songwriters were using pessimism and sarcasm as a vehicle of protest or were simply dropping out politically. Melanie, the unorthodox New York troubadour, in her offbeat way may have caught the general reform malaise best. In 1973 she observed that it was as if "all these groups" had "been fighting to change things that" were "really wrong . . . and everybody had incredible energy." It was "like they fought some secret battle somewhere and nobody knows where or how but we lost and came back somehow defeated." Melanie felt that her generation was in the throes of "an after-depression" and she was resigned "to a time of low energy for awhile."[13]

One obvious factor in protest music's decline was the collapse of student activism at the end of the 1960s. The collapse was necessarily exaggerated since the rise of campus activism had also been wildly exaggerated. There remained a substantial number of white, middle-class college youths anxious to turn America away from military adventurism abroad and corporate domination at home, yet increasingly their pillars of support were undermined. The Black, Chicano, and Indian movements drew away lower-class ethnic support and Women's Liberation drew away women, while general frustration eroded their own ranks. The Vietnam war refused to end; the campuses and cities became quiet, if not subdued; and the silent majority not only refused to shut up, they elected two of their own sons, Richard Nixon and Spiro Agnew, to rule over the new peaceable kingdom. Some of the more militant radicals went underground after a brief fling with violence; the peaceful activists either dropped out to meditate, started working for George McGovern, or slipped into more cosmic causes such as organic foods. Yippie leader Jerry Rubin discovered he had been sexist; Vietnam mobilization leader Rennie Davis found that a Maharishi had the answer to life's problems; SDS founder Tom Hayden married the radical Hollywood actress Jane Fonda. The young generation of the 1960s, brought up on contemporary protest and visions of a new world, had grown old and disillusioned. The next generation had long hair and blue jeans but shared little else with their predecessors. The younger kids grooved on music, concerts, and festivals as much as the last generation, but they were uninterested in cosmic meaning or even national problems. They would not mind having a Woodstock experience, they were enthusiastically for peace, and ostensibly for giving blacks an equal chance, but somehow these things were not their job. If reforms came, fine, but like the generation of the 1950s, the youth of the 1970s were generally content just to get along. The new stress was on observation rather than participation.

Suddenly middle-class youth's need to identify with the downtrodden masses had disappeared and with it a chief rationale for folk-protest. Folk music had always been the music of the masses. In an agrarian economy, it was the peasant's music; in an industrial society, it was the music of the worker. Folk music often contained subtle lower-class protests, but the more blatant folk-protest was always a middle-class effort to identify with the socially oppressed. Folk-protest was a way of being a witness for righteousness. Once this relationship was solidly established in the late 1950s, the folk-protest singers became leaders of a tight conspiratorial movement. Within the subversive, righteous atmosphere that permeated their performances, it mattered not what songs they sang. There, a simple patriotic song like "God Bless America" could take on the colorings of a radical hymn. Precisely because middle-class youth had no problems, they wanted to feel pain. After 1966, when youth began to feel itself a separate and somewhat oppressed class, in an era of slurs against long hair and the Vietnam draft, proletarian protest became a peripheral issue, pushed aside by the youth revolution.

There was increasingly less interest in arguing about what song lyrics meant. For example, the so-called "Dylanologists" lost their audience. The youth did not seek meaning but mystique. Simultaneously they searched for an all-encompassing oneness and individuality. They dropped out of a conformist establishment society only to fall into a rigidly nonconformist youth culture. Faced with such contradictory aims, it was better not to talk about meaning. Since the now generation had the illusion of unanimity, trying to define what they agreed on was more likely to produce division than accord. For each individual, it was enough that the music filled a personal need.

Nevertheless, if the songs became less important, the folk

writer-performers themselves became more important as models for youth obsessed with individuality. Traditionally, the folksinger was a brawny laborer, an ex-convict, a hobo, or perhaps a college-educated amateur folklorist. The contemporary folksinger, however, was more likely an alienated college dropout or graduate, seeking self-identity, money, or both through his music. More importantly, many singers symbolized personal integrity. Youth felt that Joan Baez, Phil Ochs, or Bob Dylan could not be bought in the traditional, show-business sense. Thus, even though Bob Dylan renounced protest music, he remained popular with practically all young radicals, because he consistently functioned as a social rebel and refused to bow to the press, or fans, or musical fads. Many preached doing your own thing, but Dylan lived it. He thus remained a credible existential hero.

Yet another factor in the decline of protest music was the impossible expectations that folk fans had for their folksinger-heroes. Inevitably the singers became victims of their own legend. Rock stars in general, and folk-protest singers in particular, constantly were called upon to match their new music to their inflated reputations. For example, during Bob Dylan's triumphant 1974 tour *Newsweek* quoted a record company executive who claimed that the tour was "the biggest of its kind in the history of show business." A young fan was quoted as believing that Dylan was "the most important musician who ever lived—more important than Beethoven." And Ralph Gleason breezily stated that Dylan's "impact . . . upon the culture of the past ten years in the English-speaking world" was comparable in terms of "concepts and additions to the language, only with Shakespeare and the Bible."[14] But activist entertainers were caught in a double bind. Not only were they expected to be super performers, but also extraordinary public leaders. As social reformers they were encouraged to pose as experts on social problems.

There are some obvious dangers when artists assume public leadership. Not the least is that they may be corrupted by power or its illusion. In *The Best and the Brightest*, David Halberstam brilliantly pointed out how a combination of power and confidence led many of John Kennedy's competent advisors to indulge their arrogance and assume expertise in areas foreign to their specialties. Indeed, despite the many failures of various specialists outside their fields of competence, Americans are still vulnerable to the claims of the all-around expert. Arthur Herzog, in his book *The B. S. Factor*, labels this modern Renaissance Man "the anything authority." Such a person has credentials in one field accepted as valid in other fields, one of which is usually politics. Recent examples include biologist George Wald, pediatrician Benjamin Spock, and chemist Linus Pauling. Naturally, folk-protest singers often functioned as "anything authorities." As Herzog notes, the trouble with an "anything authority" is not that he takes positions or works for causes, "but that he seldom seems to apply the same standards of research and documentation to the field in which he is not an expert that he would to his own."[15] The entire syndrome is based on the hope that someone still knows something of value outside his narrow field, despite mountains of evidence to the contrary. Thus, a folk-protest star probably would not discuss music in the glib way that he might discuss ecology, racism, and politics. Yet, Herzog's thesis should be viewed only as a caution and not as an axiom of public leadership, since the political system will not function unless specialists take pains to become expert on politics and speak out on public issues. Despite their necessary shallowness on some issues, the folk-protest singers should be congratulated for their public interest and general knowledgeability. Indeed, the avowed purpose of their protest songs was to get people interested in issues and not to supply solutions. Yet in the process it was perhaps inevitable that these singers would become bigger-than-life heroes, endowed with supposedly extraordinary powers of perception.

Naturally all this hero worship, mystique, and charisma were big business, and with the expanding youth market, very profitable. Indeed, commercialism was the one charge that all folk heroes must avoid. Some social reformers, however, did not fear the dangers of the marketplace; rather they welcomed the struggle for the youth market. Others thought that commercialism had killed protest music by making it more profitable for songs to be bland, general, and technically pleasing. Too often conviction could be compromised by the promise of money and fame. At the same time, amid all the glitter, the audience might see the songs simply as entertainment. In 1967 Julius Lester, a bitter, black topical song writer, put it this way, "I understand that Woody [Guthrie] carved 'This Machine Kills Fascists' on the top of his guitar. Maybe his did. Mine didn't. The fascists just applauded me."[16]

However, the question was never whether protest music was alive and well commercially. The influence of protest music could not be measured statistically, for the few it affected might be particularly vigorous activists who influenced many others. The real problem was that protest music had been fragmented by its commercial success, cultural acceptance, and failure to establish new relationships with specific social reform movements. Increasingly, the most gifted topical writers and singers were striking out in several directions for personal reasons.

By 1970 the folk revival and its offspring, the protest song renaissance, had not died, but both were badly disintegrated. Perhaps this was appropriate in an age of polarization, fragmentation, and general discord. Yet those who mourn the decline of protest music can find solace in the effervescent wisdom of that perennial optimist, Pete Seeger. Back in 1965, Seeger celebrated the miraculous revival of social concern among youth in contrast to declining worker and union reform activity. In closing he described an historical cycle that could give hope to the most disheartened reformer:

> History shows that there is a hidden heritage of militancy which comes and goes, but never completely dies. It under-

goes transformations and permutations from century to century, but the lessons learned by one generation, even though in defeat, are passed on to the next. Right now, many of the song traditions of the 1930s are seeing new life as never before—in the freedom songs of the South and in the topical singers of many a campus.[17]

The eternal cycle that Seeger suggested may be ready for another round. In the early 1960s, topical songs were needed to bring youth face to face with specific evils and strengthen group solidarity, for if you were affluent enough to be free from physical oppression, you had to feel oppression metaphorically. Somewhat later, when topical music became more common and somewhat monotonous, the abstract protest songs pioneered by Bob Dylan and institutionalized in many folk-rock numbers served a useful purpose. They reached young people so turned off from society that they could not see the forest for the trees. Today's youth are more likely lost in the forest and unable to isolate specific social concerns. What protest music needs is another young Bob Dylan—not an entertainer with good voice inflections and a perfected musical style, but an artist with specific social visions. No doubt folk-protest advocates have long since stopped waiting for the old Dylan to lead some new renaissance; more likely they are waiting for some new Dylan to start another cycle.

The folk-protest singers were heroes largely because they somehow managed to thumb their noses at a corrupt society, while rising to fame and fortune. They took on the whole monolithic system and flourished on the struggle. Thus, it became easier and easier for youth to accept these clearly potent individuals as spokesmen. Easier, for example, to accept Joan Baez's 1964 announcement that "Bob Dylan says what a lot of people my age feel, but cannot say."[18] The crucial thing for these cultural heroes was that they not appear too eager to please, that they appeal to the righteous few rather than to the decadent mass audience. For if they were too popular, by definition, they spoke to and for everybody and therefore nobody.

The folk-protest era is gone, but the memories and legends linger. The generation that came of age between 1955 and 1970 will always identify social protest with a lone guitar-strumming figure, bringing both bad news and high hopes with measured beat and traditional folk style. New protest singers will inevitably come forth in some new age of social activism to replace these minstrels of the dawn, but for now they remain the legendary masters of folk-protest. Woody Guthrie did it earliest and most convincingly, Pete Seeger did it longest, Joan Baez did it most artfully, Phil Ochs tried the hardest, and the young Bob Dylan did it best. If their new dawn never really came, it seems fair to say they at least helped to stave off that final night they warned of between the lines of their songs.

Notes

INTRODUCTION (FOLK MUSIC, PROTEST, AND CULTURAL HEROES)

[1]Gene Lees, "The Folk-Music Bomb," *Hi/Fi Stereo Review* (November 1964), quoted in Donald Myrus, *Ballads, Blues, and the Big Beat* (New York, 1966), p. 28.

[2]Paul Nelson and John Panake, "P-for-Protesty," *Little Sandy Review* 25 (April 1962), 8-9.

[3]On the connection between folk music and the left, especially see R. Serge Denisoff, *Great Day Coming: Folk Music and the American Left* (Urbana, 1972).

[4]Dick Reuss, "So You Want to be a Folklorist?" *Sing Out!* 15 (November 1965), 40.

[5]On this point see Daniel J. Boorstin, *The Americans: The Democratic Experience* (New York, 1973), pp. 306-447.

[6]*Time*, June 1, 1962, p. 40.

[7]"Just Playin Folks," *Saturday Evening Post*, May 30, 1964, p. 25.

[8]For a suggestive view of the nature of celebrities, see Daniel J. Boorstin, *The Image: Or What Happened to the American Dream* (New York, 1961), pp. 45-76. For a comprehensive anthology on the changing nature of heroes see Harold Lubin (editor), *Heroes and Anti-Heroes* (San Francisco, 1968).

[9]Speech by David Harris, recorded on Joan Baez record album, *Carry It On* (Vanguard Records, 1971).

[10]Christopher Lasch, *The New Radicalism in America, 1889-1963* (New York, 1965), especially see pp. 286-349.

Chapter 1 (The Evolution of the American Protest Song)

[1]On this point see Daniel J. Boorstin, *The Americans: The National Experience* (New York, 1965), pp. 190-199. For the best general history of American protest songs, see John Greenway, *American Folksongs of Protest* (Philadelphia, 1953).

[2]Quoted by Irwin Silber, monthly column in *Sing Out!* 15 (April-May 1965), 40.

[3]*Ibid.*, p. 41.

[4]Richard Brazier, "The Story of I. W. W.'s *Little Red Songbook*," *Labor History* 9 (Winter 1965), 97

[5]Reprinted from *I. W. W. Songs*, 32nd Edition (Chicago, by Ralph Chaplin, 1968), p. 10.

[6]Pete Seeger, "What Ever Happened to Singing in the Unions," *Sing Out!* 15 (May 1965), 29.

[7]Woody Guthrie, *Bound for Glory* (New York, 1943), p. 232.

[8]Woody Guthrie (edited by Robert Shelton), *Born to Win* (New York, 1965), p. 223.

[9]On the career of the Almanac Singers see Gordon Friesen, "The Almanac Singers," *Broadside* 8 (June 1962); 9 (July 1962); and 15 (November 1962) On the goals and aims of the People's Songs group, see R. Serge Denisoff, "Urban Folk 'Movement' Research: Value Free?," *Western Folklore* 28 (July 1969), 183-197; "The Proletarian Renascence: The Folkness of the Ideological Folk," *Journal of American Folklore* 82 (January 1969), 51-65. On the general topic of folk music and the political left, R. Serge Denisoff's excellent *Great Day Coming: Folk Music and the American Left* (Urbana, 1971) is indispensable.

[10]*People's Songs Bulletin 3* (February-March 1948) 2-4. The song, "The Gol-dern Red," copyright *Sing Out!*, 1948. Used by permission.

[11]Quoted in Oscar Brand, *The Ballad Mongers* (New York, 1962), p. 128.

[12]*People's Songs Bulletin* 2 (December 1947), 2.

[13]*Red Channels: The Report of Communist Influence in Radio and Television* (New York, 1950). Counterattack's subtitle was *The Newsletter of Facts to Combat Communism.*

[14]Theodore Bikel, "They Are My People," *Liberation* 7 (October 1963), 5.

[15]Pete Seeger's column in *Sing Out!* 19 (December-January 1969), 39.

[16]*Newsweek,* November 27, 1961, p. 84.

[17]Quoted in *Little Sandy Review* 13 (April 1961), 3-5.

[18]Pete Seeger, "The Theory of Cultural Guerilla Tactics," *Sing Out!* 11 (October-November 1961), 60.

CHAPTER 2 (THE NEW REVIVALISM: PROTEST MUSIC AS A RELIGIOUS EXPERIENCE)

[1]"Interview with Roger McGuinn of the Byrds," *Sing Out!* 18 (December 1968), 11.

[2]David A. Noebel, *Rhythm, Riots and Revolution* (Tulsa, 1966) and *Communism, Hypnotism and the Beatles* (Tulsa, 1965).

[3]Alfred G. Aronowitz and Marshall Blonsky, "Three's Company," *Saturday Evening Post,* May 30, 1964, p. 32. Interestingly enough, the trio did use their power by joining Eugene McCarthy's 1968 presidential campaign.

[4]Timothy Leary, "Thank God for the Beatles," in *The Beatles Book,* edited by Edward F. David (New York, 1968), p. 50.

[5]Jeremy Collier, *A Short View of the Immorality and Profaneness of the English State* (London, 1698), Introduction.

[6]Jowett translation, Plato, *The Republic,* 3rd ed., Book IV, 424c,d,e (New York, 1928), p. 146.

[7]Pete Seeger, regular column in *Sing Out!* 18 (December 1968), 39.

[8]On the relationship between the civil rights movement and protest songs see Josh Dunson, *Freedom in the Air* (New York, 1965). On the role of *People's Songs, Broadside,* and *Sing Out!,* see Dick Reuss, "Topical Songs from *People's Songs* to *Broadside:* The Changing Times," *Broadside* 55 (February 12, 1965) and R. Serge Denisoff, "Protest Movements: Class Consciousness and the Propa-

ganda Song," *Sociological Quarterly* 9 (1968); "Urban Folk 'Movement' Research: Value Free?" *Western Folklore* 27 (July 1969).

[9]"Interview with Roger McGuinn of the Byrds," p. 12.

[10]Jon Panake and Paul Nelson, "P-for-Protesty," *Little Sandy Review* 25 (April 1962), 17.

[11]Simon Kunen, *The Strawberry Statement* (New York, 1969), p. 113.

[12]Ric Masten's "The Protest Biz," copyright 1967 by Mastenville Music Publishing (BMI). Used by permission.

[13]Irwin Silber, "Country Joe Unstrung," *Sing Out!* 18 (June 1968), 71, 73.

[14]"Interview with Phil Ochs," *Broadside* 63 (October 15, 1965), 5-7.

[15]Woody Guthrie (edited by Robert Shelton), *Born to Win* (New York, 1965), pp. 222-223.

[16]Quoted in John Greenway, *American Folksongs of Protest* (Philadelphia, 1953), p. 289.

CHAPTER 3 (CONVERTING THE MASSES: POPULAR MUSIC AS A RADICAL INFLUENCE)

[1]*The American College Dictionary* (New York, 1966).

[2]For an interesting discussion of the intellectual meaning of radicalism, see Daniel Boorstin, "The New Barbarians," *Esquire* (October 1968), pp. 159-162. For an English view of American radicalism, see T. B. Bottomore, *Critics of Society: Radical Thought in North America* (New York, 1966).

[3]George Cornell, "Radicals for Jesus Make Campus Scene," Associated Press story in *Fort Worth Star-Telegram*, June 13, 1970, p. 16.

[4]Frank Kofsky, "Frank Zappa Interview," in *The Age of Rock*, edited by Jonathan Eisen (New York, 1969), pp. 255-256.

[5]Malvina Reynolds, letter to editor in *Broadside* 83 (August 1967), 7.

[6]"Country Joe Unstrung," *Sing Out!* 18 (June 1968), 20-21.

[7]Ralph J. Gleason, "Like a Rolling Stone," in Eisen, *The Age of Rock*, p. 72. Also see Alan Coren, "Head Stone," *Playboy* (November 1969), pp. 162-164.

[8]For a brilliant study of culturally alienated youth see Kenneth Kenniston, *The Uncommitted* (New York, 1960).

[9]Bottomore, *Critics of Society*, p. 101.

[10]Theodore Roszak, *The Making of a Counter Culture* (New York, 1969); R. Serge Denisoff and Mark H. Levine, "Mannheim's Problem of Generations and Counter Culture: A Study in the Ideology of Music." (Paper presented at the 1970 Pacific Sociological Association Annual Meeting). Also, for a perceptive critique of Roszak's work, see Michael Lerner, "Anarchism and the American Counter Culture," *Government and Opposition* 5 (Autumn 1970), 430-445.

[11]Note that in 1969 a radical student group at Indiana University published a "disorientation booklet" for freshmen to compete with the official orientation pamphlet.

[12]David Noebel, *Rhythm, Riots, and Revolution* (Tulsa, 1966); *Communism, Hypnotism, and the Beatles* (Tulsa, 1965).

[13]Noebel, *Rhythm, Riots, and Revolution*, pp. 21, 146.

[14]*Ibid.*, pp. 176, 196, 212.

[15]*New York Times*, September 15, 1970. Linkletter made his comment October 24, 1969, before the House Select Committee on Illegal Drugs, after the drug-induced death of his daughter (UPI story in *Fort Worth Press*, December 7, 1969).

[16]A good selection of rock lyrics is contained in *Rock Is Beautiful: An Anthology of American Lyrics*, edited by Stephanie Spinner (New York, 1970).

[17]R. Serge Denisoff, "Songs of Persuasion: A Sociological Analysis of Urban Propaganda Songs," *Journal of American Folklore* 79 (October, December 1966), 581-588; "Protest Movements: Class Consciousness and the Propaganda Song," *Sociological Quarterly* 9 (1968), 228-247.

[18]Handbill distributed at the University of Texas at Arlington, February 18, 1970.

[19]Letter to *Newsweek* editor from Sue Griffin, printed in *Newsweek* March 17, 1969, p. 6.

[20]See John Lennon's and Paul McCartney's "The Word," reproduced in *Journey to Freedom*, edited by Landon Gerald Downey (Chicago, 1969), p. 30.

[21]Kunen quoted from interview on CBS television show, "Camera Three," July 12, 1970. Frank Zappa has a similar view in Kofsky, "Frank Zappa Interview," p. 257.

[22]Tom Paxton quoted Glen Campbell in "An Interview with Tom Paxton," *Broadside* 67 (February 1966), 8. Tom Paxton, "Folk Rot," *Sing Out!* 15 (January 1966), 103. Paxton noted, although rock versions of Bob Dylan's integrationist ballad, "Blowin' in the Wind,"

were danced to in many a "lily-white" Southern fraternity house, there was "no rush to sign up Negro brothers."

[23]Irwin Silber, "The Cultural Retreat," *The Guardian*, December 6, 1969, p. 17. Also see Irwin Silber, "Fan the Flames," *Sing Out!* 18 (March 1968), 39.

[24]Emerson Hunsberger Loucks, *Ku Klux Klan in Pennsylvania: A Study in Nativism* (New York, 1936), p. 122. See also Marcello Truzzi, "Folksongs on the Right," *Sing Out!* 13 (October 1963), 51, 53.

[25]Song, "Kosher Christmas," reproduced in letter to *Sing Out!* 12 (April 1962), 59.

[26]On this point see R. Serge Denisoff, "Kent State, Muskogee, and the White House," *Broadside* 108 (July 1970), 2-4.

[27]For examples of antipollution songs see *The Sierra Club Survival Songbook* (New York, 1971). For examples of women's liberation songs see the women's music quarterly, *Paid My Dues*, initiated in 1973 and devoted to music by and about women.

[28]Quoted in transcript of symposium of protest songs in Havana, Cuba in *Sing Out!* 17 (October 1967), 30.

[29]Buffy St. Marie quoted on CBS television show "Camera Three," August 30, 1970.

[30]Quoted in "Changes in Today's College Students," *U.S. News and World Report*, February 17, 1964, p. 67.

[31]Paul Goodman, *New York Times Magazine*, February 25, 1968, p. 6.

[32]"Country Joe Unstrung," p. 19.

[33]Pete Seeger, quoted in his column in *Sing Out!* 18 (June 1968), 85.

[34]John F. Kennedy, quoted in *Sing Out!* 16 (February 1966), 80.

CHAPTER 4 (WOODY GUTHRIE: A FATHER OF THE NOW GENERATION)

[1]Woody Guthrie (edited by Robert Shelton), *Born to Win* (New York, 1965), p. 223.

[2]Woody Guthrie's life, from his birth to 1942, is vividly traced in his autobiography, *Bound for Glory* (New York, 1943). Additional information on his earlier life, along with comments on his career during and after World War Two, is found in Woody Guthrie, "My Life," in *American Folksong*, edited by Moses Asch (New York, 1961).

[3]Guthrie, "My Life," p. 3.

[4]Guthrie, *Bound for Glory*, pp. 231, 232.

[5]Guthrie, "My Life," p. 3.

[6]*Ibid.*, p. 4.

[7]*Ibid.*, p. 5.

[8]*Ibid.*, pp. 6-7.

[9]Guthrie, *Born to Win*, pp. 222-223.

[10]Quoted in Donald Myrus, *Ballads, Blues and the Big Beat* (New York, 1966), p. 45.

[11]Quoted in "Woody's Boy," *Newsweek*, May 23, 1966, p. 113.

[12]Quoted in *Sing Out!* 16 (December-January 1967-1968), 5.

[13]*Ibid.*, p. 4.

[14]Pete Seeger, "Woody Guthrie and the Gift to Be Simple," *Little Sandy Review* 5 (August 1960), 20.

[15]Remarks quoted in an advertisement for McDonald's record, *Country Joe McDonald Thinking of Woody Guthrie*, in *Rolling Stone*, November 20, 1969, p. 9.

[16]Woody Guthrie, *Born to Win*, pp. 162-163.

[17]Irwin Silber's column in *Sing Out!* 16 (December-January 1967-1968), 55.

[18]*Ibid.*

[19]David A. Noebel, *Rhythm, Riots, and Revolution* (Tulsa, 1966), pp. 134-136. Richard Reuss, a Guthrie scholar, argues there is no evidence that Guthrie was actually a Communist Party member. However, he was obviously very sympathetic to the American Communist Party. On this point see R. Serge Denisoff, *Great Day Coming: Folk Music and the American Left* (Urbana, 1971), p. 137.

[20]Pete Seeger, "Woody Guthrie—Some Reminiscences," *Sing Out!* 14 (July 1964), 26-28.

[21]Paxton quoted in Gordon Friesen, "Something New Has Been Added," *Sing Out!* 13 (October-November 1963), 16.

[22]Woody's early albums, especially for Folkway Records, never sold well. However, since 1960 several companies have released collections of his previously recorded songs. One of the best and most representative collections is the two-record album, *The Greatest Songs of Woody Guthrie* (Vanguard Records, 1970). The album includes Guthrie songs sung by Woody and interpreted by such singers as Jack Elliott, Cisco Houston, The Weavers, and Joan Baez.

[23]Woody Guthrie, Alan Lomax, and Pete Seeger, *Hard Hitting Songs for Hard-Hit People* (New York, 1967). A collection of 150 songs from the 1920s and 1930s.

[24]Paul Nelson, "Newport: Down There on a Visit," *Little Sandy Review* 30 (September 1962), 51.

[25]For a comprehensive, if uneven, treatment of Guthrie's

influence on Dylan, see Anthony Scaduto, *Bob Dylan: An Intimate Biography* (New York, 1971), especially pp. 39-54, 56-57, 62-67, 78-86. Scaduto's book is based almost entirely on the comments of people who knew Dylan personally.

[26]*Ibid.*, p. 57.

[27]Pete Seeger, "Woody Guthrie and the Gift to Be Simple," p. 20.

[28]For this interpretation of Lincoln, see Richard Hofstadter, *The American Political Tradition* (New York, 1948), pp. 93-95.

[29]Milton Okun, *Something to Sing About* (New York, 1967), p. 17.

[30]Silber quoted in *Broadside*, 118 (March-April 1972), 4.

[31]Friesen quoted in *Ibid.*

[32]John Greenway, "Woody Guthrie: The Man, The Land, The Understanding," in *The American Folk Scene*, edited by David A. De Turk and A. Poulin, Jr. (New York, 1967), pp. 184-202.

[33]Denisoff, *Great Day Coming*, pp. 97-99, 135-137.

[34]Lilian Roxon, *Lilian Roxon's Rock Encyclopedia* (New York, 1969), p. 214.

Chapter 5 (Phil Ochs: A Minstrel's Search for Martyrdom)

[1]Quoted in Anthony Scaduto, *Bob Dylan: An Intimate Biography* (New York: Grosset and Dunlap, 1971), p. 229.

[2]Peter Schjeldahl, "Phil Ochs: Kipling of the New Left," in Ray B. Browne and David Madden (editors), *The Popular Culture Explosion* (Iowa City, 1972), p. 70. The article was originally published by *Avant Garde* in 1968.

[3]*Ibid.*

[4]*Ibid.* Also see the short biographical sketch of Ochs in Milt Okun, *Something to Sing About* (New York, 1968), p. 198, and also in Gordon Friesen's, "Something New Has Been Added," *Sing Out!* 13 (October-November 1963), 19.

[5]Quoted in Schjeldahl, p. 73.

[6]Phil Ochs, *I Ain't Marching Anymore* (Elektra Records, 1965).

[7]Ochs, *Phil Ochs in Concert* (Elektra Records, 1966).

[8]Ochs, *I Ain't Marching Anymore* (liner notes).

[9]Ochs, "The Need for Topical Music," *Broadside* 22 (March 1963), 1-2.

[10]Editorial comment, *Broadside* 24 (April 1963), 13. Ochs's seventeen songs appeared from March 1962 to June 1963.

[11]"Topical Songs and Folksinging, 1965: A Symposium," in *The American Folk Scene*, edited by David A. De Turk and A. Poulin, Jr. (New York, 1967), pp. 153-155. Other symposium participants were Don West, Ewan MacColl, Chad Mitchell, John Cohen, Josh Dunson, and Moses Asch. They viewed the future of topical music in more traditional political terms.

[12]Ochs, "An Open Letter from Phil Ochs to Irwin Silber, Paul Wolfe and Joseph R. Levine," *Broadside* 54 (January 1965), 11-12.

[13]See especially Ochs, "Son of 'My Back Pages,' " *Broadside* 57 (April 1965), 13; and "An Interview with Phil Ochs," *Broadside* 63 (October 1965), 3-7.

[14]"An Interview with Phil Ochs," p. 6.

[15]Scaduto, p. 176.

[16]"An Interview with Phil Ochs," p. 7.

[17]Paul Wolfe, review of *I Ain't Marching Anymore*, *Broadside* 57 (April 1965), 13-14.

[18]West quoted in "Topical Songs and Folksinging: A Symposium," p. 150.

[19]Nat Hentoff, "The Future of the Folk Renascence," in *The American Folk Scene*, p. 330.

[20]Ochs, *The War Is Over* (New York, 1969), p. 44.

[21]Ochs, *Pleasures of the Harbor* (A & M Records, 1967).

[22]For a detailed look at Dylan's artistic progression between 1965 and 1968, see Scaduto, pp. 187-249.

[23]Ochs quoted in "What They're Saying," *Sing Out!* 16 (February-March 1966), 85.

[24]Ochs, "Have You Heard? The War Is Over," *Village Voice*, November 23, 1967, p. 4.

[25]"Interview with Phil Ochs, Part I," *Broadside* 89 (February-March 1968), 11, 12.

[26]"Interview with Phil Ochs, Part II," *Broadside* 90 (April 1968), 7.

[27]"Interview with Phil Ochs, Part III," *Broadside* 91 (May 1968), 8.

[28]Jac Holzman, Letter in *Broadside* 92 (June 1968), 12.

[29]*New York Times*, May 20, 1968.

[30]*Village Voice* report quoted in *Broadside* 94 (September-October 1968), 10.

[31]Ochs, *Tape from California* (A & M Records, 1968).

[32]Ochs, "Sing Out" column, *Village Voice*, July 21, 1966, p. 6.

[33]Ochs, *Rehearsals for Retirement* (A & M Records, 1969).

[34]Ochs, *Phil Ochs' Greatest Hits* (A & M Records, 1970).

[35]*Broadside*, 116 (November 1971), 3.

[36]Jerry Rubin, *We Are Everywhere* (New York, 1972), pp. 238-240.

[37]*Broadside* 120 (August 1972), 3. This issue was printed three months late.

[38]*Ibid.*

[39]Lasch quoted in William Braden, *The Age of Aquarius* (New York, 1971), p. 50.

[40]"Crucifixion" appears on Ochs's album *The Pleasures of the Harbor* (Elektra Records, 1967).

Chapter 6 (Joan Baez: A Pacifist St. Joan)

[1]Her tax protests were only symbolic. The Internal Revenue Department simply attached her bank account and collected not only her total tax bill, but additional penalty interest. For her original reasons for her tax protest, see her letter to The Internal Revenue Service, reprinted in *Sing Out!* 14 (June 1964), 12.

[2]The Institute is now in its seventh year of operation. For a witty look at the early Institue, see Joan Didion, "Just Folks at a School for Nonviolence," *New York Times Magazine*, February 27, 1966.

[3]For biographical data on Baez's early years, most writers rely on Time's research staff. See their feature article on Joan, "Sibyl with Guitar," November 23, 1962, pp. 54-56. For much more detailed, though incomplete, information, see Joan Baez's semi-autobiographical *Daybreak* (New York, 1968), especially, pp. 1-66.

[4]Interview with Joan Baez, Dan Wakefield, "I'm Really a Square," *Redbook* (January 1967), p. 115.

[5]Baez, *Daybreak*, pp. 40, 42, 48-49. Joan added that since 1947, her father "never accepted a job that had anything to do with armaments, offense, defense, or whatever they prefer to call it."

[6]*Ibid.*, p. 40.

[7]"To Prison with Love," *Time*, December 11, 1964, p. 60. Folksinger Phil Ochs was also involved in the Free Speech Movement at Berkeley.

[8]Joan Baez, "With God on Our Side," *Liberation* 10 (August 1965), 35.

[9]Robert Simple, "Vietnam Critics Stage Sit-Down at White House," *New York Times*, August 7, 1965.

[10]Peter Braestrup, "Joan Baez and the Interpreter, or What the Japanese Didn't Hear," *New York Times*, February 21, 1967; Editorial, *Sing Out!* 17 (April 1967), 1.

[11]Baez, *Daybreak*, pp. 31-35; "Caroling Joan Baez, Mother Arrested at War Protest," UPI dispatch in *Dallas Morning News*, December 20, 1967.

[12]For an account of David and Joan's antiwar activities before he entered prison, see *Daybreak*, pp. 149-157 and Nat Hentoff's excellent "Playboy Interview: Joan Baez," *Playboy* (July 1970), pp. 54-62+. Also, a documentary film, *Carry It On*, which covered their campus tours in 1968 and 1969 was released in 1970. Baez and David Harris have been legally separated since 1972 because of personal problems, but they remain on good terms and are still committed to the same type of pacifism.

[13]"The Dick Cavett Show," August 4, 1969. Howard K. Smith, quoted on "The ABC Evening News," August 5, 1969. Baez's earlier appearances were "The Alan Burke Show," October 28, 1967, and "The Les Crane Show," August 30, 1968. She also was a guest on "The David Frost Show" with son Gabriel, June 20, 1970. All comments are based on audio tapes of the television shows.

[14]Quoted in *Newsweek*, September 14, 1970, p. 65.

[15]News story, *Fort Worth Star-Telegram*, February 4, 1971.

[16]Jack O'Brian, column in *Fort Worth Star-Telegram*, February 23, 1971. This had always been a problem when she toured with her husband. Crowds came to hear her sing and were impatient with David's philosophical harangues.

[17]Quoted on "The Dick Cavett Show," February 9, 1971, and "The David Frost Show," March 12, 1971.

[18]Richard Fariña, "Baez and Dylan: A Generation Singing Out," in *The American Folk Scene*, edited by David A. De Turk and A. Poulin, Jr. (New York, 1967), p. 253. The article was originally printed in *Mademoiselle* in March, 1964.

[19]The Institute regularly announced its activities through a *Newsletter* available on request. Its views are most explicit perhaps in the brief pamphlets it distributes, such as Emile Copouye, *Laying Down the Gun*, David Harris, *The Big Lie Technique*, and Henry Anderson, *The Denaturalization of Human Nature*. On the establishment of the Institute see Dave A. De Turk and A. Poulin, Jr., "Joan Baez: An Interview," in *The American Folk Scene*, pp. 231-249; Baez, *Daybreak*, pp. 56-76.

[20]David Harris, *Goliath* (New York, 1970).

[21]Baez, *Daybreak*, p. 136.

[22]Hentoff, "Playboy Interview: Joan Baez," p. 54.

23Baez, *Daybreak*, p. 77.

24Paul Nelson and Jon Panake, "Record Reviews," *Little Sandy Review* 18 (September 1961), 3-6.

25Alan Weberman and Gordon Friesen, "Joan Baez and the Bob Dylan Songs," *Broadside* 97 (March 1969), 1-2, 9-10.

26Her early albums (all recorded by Vanguard) were *Joan Baez* (1960), *Joan Baez, Volume 2* (1961), *Joan Baez in Concert* (1962), *Joan Baez in Concert, Part 2* (1962), *Joan Baez 5* (1963), *Farewell Angeline* (1965), and *Noel* (1966).

27Quoted in Dan Wakefield, "I'm Really a Square," p. 123.

28Her last seven albums on Vanguard were *Joan* (1967), *Baptism* (1968), *Any Day Now* (1969), *David's Album* (1969), *One Day at a Time* (1970), *Joan Baez: The First Ten Years* (1970), and *Blessed Are* (1971). *Come from the Shadows* was recorded and released in 1972 and *Where Are You Now, My Son?* in 1973 by A & M Records.

29Nat Hentoff, "Jazz and Pop '72," *Playboy* (February 1972), pp. 211-212

30Daniel J. Boorstin, *The Image: Or What Happened to the American Dream* (New York, 1961), pp. 45-76.

31Quoted in Dan Wakefield, "I'm Really a Square," p. 120.

32Baez, *Daybreak*, pp. 42-44.

33For a typical attack on Baez's view of black power, see the editorial, *Broadside* 83 (August 1967), 8-9. For her present views on various activist groups, see Hentoff, "Playboy Interview: Joan Baez."

34David A. Noebel, *Rhythm, Riots, and Revolution* (Tulsa, 1966), pp. 202-203.

35Editorial, *Broadside* 79 (February 1967), 2.

36"The Folk Girls," *Time*, June 1, 1962, p. 39.

37"Hoots and Hollers on the Campus," *Newsweek*, November 27, 1961, p. 84.

38Quoted in Tom O'Leary, "Joan Baez—A Lesser Flop," *World Campus* 2 (December 1967), 15.

39Results of the Antioch poll reproduced in *Parade*'s "Keeping Up with Youth" column, May 28, 1972, p. 4. In the 1964 poll Gandhi still ranked first, John Kennedy was second, and though Schweitzer and King were in the top ten, so were Winston Churchill, Franklin Roosevelt, Albert Einstein, and Woodrow Wilson. The only woman on the 1964 list was Eleanor Roosevelt, who placed eighth.

40"To Prison with Love," p. 60.

CHAPTER 7 (BOB DYLAN: BEYOND LEFT AND RIGHT)

[1]Quoted in transcript of Dylan's film, *Don't Look Back*, in D. A. Pennebaker (editor), *Don't Look Back* (New York, 1968), p. 42.

[2]This attitude was very apparent in most of his interviews, especially see Jann Wenner, "The *Rolling Stone* Interview: Dylan," *Rolling Stone*, November 29, 1969, pp. 23-33.

[3]For McLuhan's view of television see Marshall McLuhan, *Understanding Media* (New York, 1964), pp. 40-48, 272-297.

[4]Dylan quoted on his youth in "Let Us Now Praise Little Men," *Time*, May 31, 1963, p. 40. By far the best source for Dylan's background and early career is Anthony Scaduto, *Bob Dylan: An Intimate Biography* (New York, 1971).

[5]Toby Thompson, *Positively Main Street* (New York, 1971). Thompson's book goes into detail on Dylan's early life and his relationship with Echo Hellstrom.

[6]The best account by far of these early years in the Village come from comments by Jack Elliott, Dave Van Ronk, Phil Ochs, and others in Scaduto, *Bob Dylan*.

[7]Suze Rotolo appears on the cover of *The Freewheelin' Bob Dylan* (Columbia Records, 1962).

[8]Previously the only Dylan song to hit the top ten charts was "Blowin' in the Wind," recorded by Peter, Paul and Mary in 1963.

[9]Large portions of the speech are quoted in Scaduto, pp. 161-162.

[10]I have drawn heavily on Scaduto's very accurate chronology for the outlines of Dylan's career.

[11]Arnold Shaw, "The New Folksingers," *Harper's* 229 (November 1964), 38.

[12]"The Angry Young Folk Singer," *Life*, April 10, 1964, p. 114.

[13]Gleason quoted in *Broadside* 44 (April 30, 1964), 12.

[14]Irwin Silber, "An Open Letter to Bob Dylan," *Sing Out!* 14 (November 1964), 22-23.

[15]Paul Wolfe, "The New Dylan," *Broadside* 53 (December 20, 1964), 11.

[16]Nat Hentoff, "The Crackin', Shakin', Breakin' Sounds," *New Yorker* 40 (October 24, 1964), 65.

[17]*Ibid.*, pp. 70-80.

[18]*Ibid.*, p. 86.

[19]Nora Ephron and Susan Edmiston, "Bob Dylan Interview" (1965) in Craig McGregor (editor), *Bob Dylan: A Retrospective* (New York, 1972), pp. 85, 87.

[20]Israel Young, "Frets and Frails" (his regular column), *Sing Out!* 15 (November 1965) 6.

[21]Sis Cunningham and Gordon Friesen, "An Interview with Phil Ochs," *Broadside* 63 (October 15, 1965), 2-4.

[22]See the very personal interview with Joan Baez about Bob Dylan in Scaduto, pp. 191-210.

[23]Joan Baez, *Daybreak* (New York, 1968), p. 83.

[24]Bob Dylan, Letter to *Broadside* in *Broadside* 38 (January 20, 1964), 9.

[25]*Ibid.*, p. 11.

[26]*Ibid.*, p. 10.

[27]*Long Island Press*, October 17, 1965, quoted in McGregor, p. 95.

[28]Joseph Haas, "Bob Dylan Talking," *Panorama*, supplement in *Chicago Daily News*, November 27, 1965, reprinted in McGregor, p. 113.

[29]Nat Hentoff, "The *Playboy* Interview: Bob Dylan," *Playboy* (March 1966), in McGregor, pp. 124-145.

[30]Jules Siegel, "Well, What Have We Here?" *Saturday Evening Post*, July 30, 1966, in McGregor, p. 146; Michael Iachetta, "Scarred Bob Dylan Is Comin' Back," in McGregor, pp. 198-199.

[31]Bob Dylan, "I Pity the Poor Immigrant," *John Wesley Harding* (Columbia Records, 1968).

[32]Alfred G. Aronowitz, "Dylan's Big Nonelectric Comeback," *Life*, February 9, 1968, p. 12.

[33]John Wesley Harding Is Bob Dylan," interview with Alan Weberman, *Broadside* 93 (July 1968), 5-8.

[34]*Ibid.*

[35]Steven Goldberg, "Bob Dylan and the Poetry of Salvation," *Saturday Review*, May 30, 1970, pp. 43-46.

[36]Jon Landau, "John Wesley Harding," *Crawdaddy* (1968) in McGregor, pp. 249-264.

[37]Paul Williams, "God Bless America," *Crawdaddy* (January 1968), reprinted in Paul Williams, *Outlaw Blues* (New York, 1969), pp. 71-72.

[38]Paul Nelson, review of *Nashville Skyline* in *Rolling Stone*, May 31, 1969, p. 22.

[39]Ed Ward, review of *New Morning* in *Rolling Stone*, October 27, 1970, p. 20.

[40]Gordon Friesen, "Welcome Back, Bob," *Broadside* 116 (November 1971), 1.

[41]Bob Dylan, *Tarantula* (New York, 1971).

[42]Bob Dylan song, "Playboys and Playgirls" in Bob Dylan, *Writings and Drawings* (New York, 1973), p. 154.

[43]Dylan's Song, "Tombstone Blues," *Ibid.*, p. 187.

[44]Pete Seeger, column in *Sing Out!* 17 (December 1967), 59.

[45]Dylan quoted in "Dylan—Rolling Again," *Newsweek*, January 14, 1974, p. 49.

[46]Ephron and Edmiston, "Bob Dylan Interview," p. 90.

[47]John Cohen and Happy Traum, "Conversations with Bob Dylan," *Sing Out!* 18 (October 1968), 67.

[48]Jann Wenner, "The *Rolling Stone* Interview: Bob Dylan," *Rolling Stone*, November 29, 1969, pp. 25-33.

[49]"Dylan—Rolling Again," p. 49.

CHAPTER 8 (THE DAY THE MUSIC DIED)

[1]Jon Panake and Paul Nelson, "P-for-Protesty," *Little Sandy Review* 25 (April 1962), 18.

[2]Irwin Silber's column in the *Guardian*, May 9, 1970, p. 7.

[3]For the Christian Crusade's views see David Noebel, *Rhythm, Riots, and Revolution* (Tulsa, 1966) and *Columbia Records: Home of Marxist Minstrels* (Tulsa, 1967). Silber's comments appear in the *Guardian*, December 6, 1969, p. 17.

[4]On the rise, style, and impact of these songs, see R. Serge Denisoff, "Kent State, Muskogee, and the White House," *Broadside* 108 (July 1970), 2-4.

[5]On Simon's songs see Robert Christgau's "Rock Lyrics Are Poetry (Maybe)," in Jonathan Eisen (ed.), *The Age of Rock* (New York, 1969), pp. 236-239. In 1970 on both the Dick Cavett and Johnny Carson television talk shows, Simon frankly commented on his random method of songwriting.

[6]"An Interview with Judy Collins," *Life*, May 2, 1969, pp. 45-46. Arlo Guthrie quoted in "Woody's Boy," *Newsweek*, May 23, 1966, p. 110.

[7]Editorial, *Broadside* 107 (June 1970), 9-10.

[8]Joni Mitchell quoted in *Newsweek* "Music Column," July

14, 1969, p. 62; Janis Ian and Tim Hardin quoted in "Sing Love, Not Protest," *Time*, February 23, 1968, p. 92; Donovan quoted in UPI Dispatch in *Fort Worth Press*, November 2, 1969.

[9]Cartoon by Charles Saxon in *New Yorker*, January 24, p. 30

[10]James Simon Kunen, *The Strawberry Statement* (New York, 1969), p. 94.

[11]Phil Ochs album, *Rehearsals for Retirement* (A & M Records, 1969).

[12]Theo Bikel's comment made at 1967 Newport Folk Festival, quoted in *Broadside* 87 (December 1967), 12.

[13]Mary Campbell, "Melanie Notes Slump in Songs of Protest," Associated Press story in *Indianapolis News*, April 12, 1973.

[14]"Dylan—Rolling Again," *Newsweek*, January 14, 1974, pp. 48-50.

[15]Arthur Herzog, *The B. S. Factor* (New York, 1973), *passim*.

[16]Julius Lester, Letter to the editor, *Broadside* 84 (September 1967), 7.

[17]Pete Seeger, "Whatever Happened to Singing in the Unions," *Sing Out!* 15 (May 1965), 31.

[18]Quoted in Craig McGregor (editor), *Bob Dylan: A Retrospective* (New York, 1972), p. 65.

Selected Bibliography

BOOKS

Ames, Russell. *The Story of American Folk Song.* New York: Grosset and Dunlap, 1955.

Baez, Joan. *Daybreak.* New York: Dial Press, 1968.

Benson, Dennis C. *The Now Generation.* Richmond, Va.: John Knox Press, 1969.

Bledsoe, Thomas. *Or We'll Hang Separately: The Highlander Idea.* Boston: Beacon Press, 1969.

Boorstin, Daniel J. *The Americans: The Democratic Experience.* New York: Random House, 1973.

———. *The Americans: The National Experience.* New York: Random House, 1965.

———. *The Decline of Radicalism: Reflections on America Today.* New York: Random House, 1970.

———. *The Image: Or What Happened to the American Dream.* New York: Atheneum, 1961.

Bottomore, T. B. *Critics of Society: Radical Thought in North America.* New York: Random House, 1966.

Braden, William. *The Age of Aquarius.* New York: Pocket Books, 1971.

Brand, Oscar. *The Ballad Mongers.* New York: Funk and Wagnalls, 1962.

Browne, Ray B. and David Madden, eds. *The Popular Culture Explosion,* Iowa City, Ia.: William C. Brown, 1972.

Chaplin, Ralph. *Wobbly.* Chicago: University of Chicago Press, 1948.

Christgau, Robert. *Any Old Way You Choose It: Rock and Other Pop Music, 1967-1973.* Baltimore: Penguin Books, 1973.

Cohn, Nik. *Rock from the Beginning.* New York: Stein and Day, 1969.

Collier, Jeremy. *A Short View of the Immorality and Profaneness of the English State.* London: n.p., 1698.

Conly, John M., ed. *The Joan Baez Songbook.* New York: Ryerson Music Publishers, Inc., 1964.

Davis, Edward F., ed. *The Beatles Book.* New York: Cowles Education Corporation, 1968.

Denisoff, R. Serge. *Great Day Coming: Folk Music and the American Left.* Urbana: University of Illinois Press, 1972.

De Turk, David A. and A. Poulin, Jr., eds. *The American Folk Scene.* New York: Dell Publishing, 1967.

Dowdey, Landon Gerald, ed. *Journey to Freedom.* Chicago: The Swallow Press, 1969.

Dunson, Josh. *Freedom in the Air.* New York: International Publishers, 1965.

Dylan, Bob. *Tarantula.* New York: Macmillan, 1971.

————. *Writings and Drawings.* New York: Alfred Knopf, 1973.

Eisen, Jonathan, ed. *The Age of Rock: Sounds of the American Cultural Revolution.* New York: Random House, 1969.

————. *The Age of Rock 2: Sights and Sounds of the American Cultural Revolution.* New York: Random House, 1970.

————. *Twenty-Minute Fandangos and Forever Changes: A Rock Bazaar.* New York: Random House, 1971.

Finklestein, Sidney. *How Music Expresses Ideas.* New York: International Publishers, 1952.

Goldman, Albert. *Freakshow.* New York: Atheneum, 1971.

Greenway, John. *American Folksongs of Protest.* Philadelphia: University of Pennsylvania Press, 1953.

Guthrie, Woody. *American Folksong.* Editor, Moses Asch. New York: Oak Publications, 1961.

_____. *Born to Win.* Editor, Robert Shelton. New York. Macmillan, 1965.

_____. *Bound for Glory.* New York: E. P. Dutton, 1943.

_____. *California to the New York Island.* New York: Oak Publications, 1960.

_____. Lomax, Alan and Seeger, Pete. *Hard Hitting Songs for Hard-Hit People.* New York: Oak Publications, 1967.

Harris, David. *Goliath.* New York: Avon Books, 1970.

Hemphill, Paul. *The Nashville Sound: Bright Lights and Country Music.* New York: Simon and Schuster, 1970.

Hentoff, Nat. *Peace Agitator.* New York: Macmillan, 1963.

Herzog, Arthur. *The B. S. Factor.* New York: Simon and Schuster, 1973.

Hofstadter, Richard. *The American Political Tradition.* New York: Random House, 1948.

Hopkins, Jerry. *The Rock Story.* New York: New American Library, 1970.

I.W.W. Songs, 32nd Edition. Chicago: Industrial Workers of the World, 1968.

Katzman, Allen, ed. *Our Time: Interviews from the East Village Other.* New York: Dial Press, 1972.

Kenniston, Kenneth. *The Uncommitted.* New York: Dell Publishing, 1960.

Kramer, Daniel. *Bob Dylan.* New York: Citadel Press, 1967.

Kunen, James S. *The Strawberry Statement.* New York: Avon Books, 1969.

Lasch, Christopher. *The New Radicalism in America, 1889-1963.* New York: Random House, 1965.

Lawless, Ray M. *Folksingers and Folksongs in America: A Handbook of Biography, Bibliography, and Discography.* New York: Duell, Sloan and Pearce, 1960.

Lipset, Seymour Martin and Wolin, Sheldon, eds. *The Berkeley Student Revolt: Facts and Interpretations.* New York: Doubleday & Company, 1965.

Lomas, Charles W. *The Agitator in American Society.* Englewood Cliffs, N.J.: Prentice-Hall, 1968.

Loucks, Emerson Hunsberger. *The Ku Klux Klan in Pennsylvania: A Study in Nativism.* New York: The Telegraph Press, 1936.

Lubin, Harold, ed. *Heroes and Anti-Heroes,* San Francisco: Chandler Publishing, 1968.

Lydon, Michael. *Rock Folk: Portraits from the Rock 'n' Roll Pantheon.* New York: Dell Publishing, 1973.

McGregor, Craig, ed. *Bob Dylan: A Retrospective.* New York: William Morrow, 1972.

McLuhan, Marshall. *Understanding Media.* New York: McGraw-Hill, 1964.

Morse, Jim and Mathews, Nancy, eds. *The Sierra Club Survival Songbook.* Rockville Centre, N.Y.: Belwin-Mills Publishing, 1971.

Myrus, Donald. *Ballads, Blues, and the Big Beat.* New York Macmillan, Jan. 1966.

Nettl, Bruno. *An Introduction to Folk Music in the United States.* Detroit: Wayne State University Press, 1960.

Noebel, David. *Columbia Records: Home of Marxist Minstrels.* Tulsa: Christian Crusade Publications, 1967.

———. *Communism, Hypnotism and the Beatles.* Tulsa: Christian Crusade Publications, 1965.

———. *Rhythm, Riots, and Revolution.* Tulsa: Christian Crusade Publications, 1966.

Ochs, Phil. *The War Is Over.* New York: Barricade Music, Inc., 1969.

Okun, Milton, *Something to Sing About.* New York: Macmillan, 1968.

Pennebaker, D. A. *Bob Dylan: Don't Look Back.* New York: Ballantine Books, 1968.

Red Channels: The Report of Communist Influence in Radio and Television, New York: American Business Consultants, 1950.

Ribakove, Sy and Barbara. *Folk-Rock: The Bob Dylan Story.* New York: Dell Publishing, 1966.

Rolling Stone Editors. *The Age of Paranoia: How the Sixties Ended.* New York: Pocket Books, 1972.

———. *The Rolling Stone Record Review.* New York: Pocket Books, 1971.

Rosenberg, Bruce A. *The Art of the American Folk Preacher.* New York: Oxford University Press, 1970.

Roszak, Theodore. *The Making of a Counter Culture.* New York: Doubleday and Co., 1969.

Roxon, Lilian. *Lilian Roxon's Rock Encyclopedia.* New York: Grosset and Dunlap, 1969.

Rubin, Jerry. *Do It!* New York: Ballantine Books, 1970.

———. *We Are Everywhere.* New York: Harper and Row, 1972.

Scaduto, Anthony. *Bob Dylan: An Intimate Biography.* New York: William Morrow, 1971.

Seeger, Pete. *The Incomplete Folksinger.* New York: Simon and Schuster, 1972.

Shaw, Arnold. *Belafonte: An Unauthorized Biography.* Philadelphia: Chilton Company, 1960.

Spinner, Stephanie, ed. *Rock Is Beautiful: An Anthology of American Lyrics.* New York: Dell Publishing, 1970.

Thompson, Toby. *Positively Main Street: An Unorthodox View of Bob Dylan.* New York: Coward, McCann, 1971.

Whitman, Wanda Willson, ed. *Songs That Changed the World.* New York: Crown Publishers, 1969.

Williams, Paul. *Outlaw Blues.* New York: E. P. Dutton, 1969.

ARTICLES

The complete runs of *Sing Out!* (from 1950 to the present) and especially of *Broadside* (from 1962 to the present) are indispensable for those interested in folk-protest music. Also particularly valuable during the limited years of their publication are the *People's Songs Bulletin, Caravan,* and *Little Sandy Review.*

Adams, Camilla. "Woody Guthrie: Man or Myth." *Broadside* 71 (June 1966), pp. 7-9, 10.

"The Angry Young Folk Singer." *Life,* April 10, 1964, pp. 109-117.

Armstrong, Dan. "Commercial Folksongs—Product of Instant Culture." *Sing Out!* 13 (January 1963), pp. 20-22.

Aronowitz, Alfred G. "Dylan's Big Nonelectric Comeback." *Life,* February 9, 1968, pp. 10-13.

———, and Blonsky, Marshall. "Three's Company." *Saturday Evening Post,* May 30, 1964, pp. 30-33.

Asch, Moses. "Folk Music—A Personal Statement." *Sing Out!* 11 (February-March 1961), pp. 26-27.

Baez, Joan. "I Do Not Believe in War." *Sing Out!* 14 (July 1964), p. 57.

——— "With God on Our Side." *Liberation* 10 (August 1965), pp. 35-66.

Barden, J.C. "Pete Seeger." *High Fidelity* 13 (January 1963), pp. 51-54.

"Behind the 'Conservative' Movement in Colleges." *U.S. News & World Report,* December 25, 1961, pp. 64-67.

Bikel, Theodore. "They Are My People." *Liberation* 7 (October 1963), pp. 5-7.

Bluestein, Gene. "Songs of the Silent Generation." *New Republic*, March 13, 1961, pp. 21-22.

Boorstin, Daniel J. "The New Barbarians." *Esquire* (October 1968), pp. 159-162.

Braden, Anne. "Highlander Folk School—The End and the Beginning." *Caravan* 17 (June-July 1959), pp. 30-31.

Braestrup, Peter. "Joan Baez and the Interpreter, or What the Japanese Didn't Hear." *New York Times*, February 21, 1967.

Browne, Ray B. and Winkelman, Donald M. "Folklore Study in Universities," *Sing Out!* 14 (September 1964), pp. 47, 49.

Brummell, O. B. "Bob Dylan—A Far Cry from Aristotle." *High Fidelity* 16 (October 1966), pp. 125-126.

Bryant, Beth. "Tom Paxton: Songwriter with a Conscience," *Sing Out!* 14 (November 1964), pp. 33, 35-36.

Brazier, Richard. "The Story of the I. W. W.'s Little Red Songbook." *Labor History* 9 (Winter 1968), pp. 91-105.

Campbell, Mary. "Melanie Notes Slump in Songs of Protest." *Indianapolis News*, April 12, 1973.

Carmon, Walt. "The Children of Bobby Dylan." *Life*, November 5, 1965, pp. 43-50.

"Changes in Today's College Students." *U.S. News and World Report*, February 17, 1964, pp. 66-69.

Clark, Sam. "Freedom Songs and the Folk Process." *Sing Out!* 14 (February-March 1964), pp. 16-17.

Christgau, Robert. "Tune Up, Turn Disestablishmentarian, Drop Out." *Life*, September 22, 1967, pp. 104-105, 174-176.

Cohen, John. "A Conversation with Janis Ian." *Sing Out!* 18 (March-April 1968), pp. 5, 7, 9.

———— "Joan Baez." *Sing Out!* 13 (Summer 1963), pp. 6-7, 8-9.

———— "The Revival." *Sing Out!* 11 (February-March 1961), pp. 22-24.

————, and Traum, Happy. *Sing Out!* 18 (October 1968), pp. 65-69.

Coren, Alan. "Head Stone." *Playboy* (November 1969), pp. 162-164.

Cornell, George. "Radicals for Jesus Make Campus Scene." *Fort Worth Star-Telegram*, June 13, 1970.

Cunningham, Sis, and Friesen, Gordon. "An Interview with Phil Ochs," *Broadside* 63 (October 15, 1965), pp. 2-4.

Danker, Frederick E. "Folksongs in the High School Classroom." *Sing Out!* 13 (February-March 1963), pp. 16-17.

Denisoff, R. Serge. "Dylan: Hero or Villain?" *Broadside* 58 (May 1965), pp. 5-6.

———— "Folk Music and the American Left: A Generational-Ideological Comparison." *British Journal of Sociology* 20 (December 1969), pp. 427-472.

———— "Kent State, Muskogee, and the White House." *Broadside* 108 (July 1970), pp. 4-5.

———— "The Proletarian Renascence: The Folkness of the Ideological Folk." *Journal of American Folklore* 82 (January-March 1969), pp. 61-65.

———— "Protest Movements: Class Consciousness and the Propaganda Song." *Sociological Quarterly* 9 (Spring 1968), pp. 228-247.

———— "Songs of Persuasion: A Sociological Analysis of Urban Propaganda Songs." *Journal of American Folklore* 70 (October-December 1966), pp. 581-585.

———— "Urban Folk 'Movement' Research: Value Free?" *Western Folklore* 27 (July 1969), pp. 183-197.

Didion, Joan. "Just Folk at a School for Nonviolence." *New York Times Magazine,* February 27, 1966, pp. 24-27.

Dunson, Josh. "Folk Music on Records—Topical Songs." *Sing Out!* 14 (July 1964), p. 93.

"Dylan—Rolling Again." *Newsweek,* January 14, 1974, pp. 44-49.

"The Folk-Girls." *Time,* June 1, 1962, pp. 39-40.

Friesen, Gordon. "Almanac Singers: End of the Road." *Broadside* 15 (November 1962), pp. 2-4.

———— "Open Door at Almanac House." *Broadside* 7 (June 1962), 3-5.

———— "Welcome Back, Bob." *Broadside* 116 (November 1971), p. 1.

———— "Winter and War Come to Almanac House." *Broadside* 8 (June 1962), pp. 2-4.

———— "Woody Guthrie: Hard Travelin." *Mainstream* (August 1963), pp. 4-11.

———— "Woody Works on His Book." *Broadside* 9 (July 1962), pp. 2-4.

Gleason, Ralph J. "The Times They Are A-Changin': The Changing Message of America's Young Folksingers." *Ramparts* (April 1965), pp. 36-48.

Goldberg, Steven. "Bob Dylan and the Poetry of Salvation." *Saturday Review,* May 30, 1970, pp. 43-46.

Gollan, Antoni E. "The Evolution of Bob Dylan." *National Review* 18 (June 28, 1966), pp. 638-639.

Greenway, John. "A Great Rebel Passes On." *Sing Out!* 10 (December-January 1960-1961), pp. 31-33.

Hemming, Roy. Controversy in Song." *Senior Scholastic,* May 8, 1963, p. 18.

Hentoff, Nat. "The Crackin', Shakin', Breakin' Sounds." *New Yorker,* October 24, 1964, pp. 64-92.

_____ "Folk Finds a Voice." *Reporter,* January 4, 1962, pp. 39-42.

_____ "Jazz and Pop '72." *Playboy* (February 1972), pp. 211-215.

_____ "The Odyssey of Woody Guthrie." *Pageant* (March 1964), pp. 103-108.

_____ "The *Playboy* Interview: Bob Dylan." *Playboy* (March 1966), pp. 41-49.

_____ "*Playboy* Interview: Joan Baez." *Playboy* (July 1970), pp. 54-62.

_____ "Recordings: 'I Read the News Today, Oh Boy," *Ramparts* 6 (November 1967), pp. 8, 10, 12.

_____ "Youth—the Oppressed Majority." *Playboy* (September 1967), pp. 136-138, 196-197.

Hinton, Sam. "To Define Contemporary Folk Music." *Sing Out!* 11 (February-March, 1961), pp. 16-17.

"Hoots and Hollers on the Campus." *Newsweek,* November 27, 1961, pp. 84-85.

"I Am My Words." *Newsweek,* November 4, 1963, pp. 94-95.

"An Interview with Judy Collins." *Life,* May 2, 1969, pp. 45-47.

"Interview with Phil Ochs." *Broadside* 63 (October 15, 1965), pp. 5-8.

"Interview with Phil Ochs, Part I." *Broadside* 89 (February-March 1968), pp. 10-14.

"Interview with Phil Ochs, Part II." *Broadside* 90 (April 1968), pp. 5-8.

"Interview with Phil Ochs, Part III." *Broadside* 91 (May 1968), pp. 6-9.

"Interview with Roger McGuinn of the Byrds." *Sing Out!* 18 (December 1968), pp. 8-14.

"An Interview with Tom Paxton." *Broadside* 67 (February 1966), pp. 7-9.

"John Wesley Harding Is Bob Dylan." *Broadside* 93 (August 1968), pp. 5-8.

"Just Playin' Folks," *Saturday Evening Post,* May 30, 1964, pp. 24-29.

"Keeping up with Youth." *Parade,* May 28, 1972, p. 4.

Keniston, Kenneth. "The Sources of Student Dissent." *Journal of Social Issues* 23 (July 1967), pp. 108-137.

Korall, Burt. "The Music of Protest." *Saturday Review,* November 16, 1968, pp. 36-37.

————. "Of Times That Are A-Changin'." *Saturday Review*, August 26, 1967, pp. 76-77.

Lees, Gene. "Newport Revisited." *High Fidelity* 17 (September 1967), pp. 20-23.

Lerner, Michael. "Anarchism and the American Counter Culture." *Government and Opposition* 5 (Autumn 1970), pp. 430-455.

"Let Us Now Praise Little Men." *Time*, May 31, 1963, p. 40.

Lindsay, Hope. "Bad Business." *Institute for the Study of Nonviolence Journal* (November 1967), p. 10.

Lloyd, A. L. "The English Folk Song Revival." *Sing Out!* 12 (April-May 1962), pp. 34-37.

Lund, Jens and Denisoff, R. Serge. "The Folk Music Revival and the Counter Culture." *Journal of American Folklore* 84 (October-December 1971), pp. 394-405.

Lyon, Peter. "The Ballad of Pete Seeger." *Holiday* 38 (July 1965), pp. 83-86.

MacColl, Ewan. "The Singer and the Audience." *Sing Out!* 14 (September 1964), pp. 18-19.

Marrs, Ernie. "The Incompleat Woody." *Broadside* 40 (February 1964), pp. 3-4.

Montgomery, Susan. "The Folk Furor." *Mademoiselle* 52 (December 1960), pp. 98-100, 117, 119.

Mooney, H.F. "Popular Music Since the 1920s: The Significance of Shifting Taste." *American Quarterly* 20 (Spring 1968), pp. 79-84.

Nelson, Paul. "Newport: Down There on a Visit." *Little Sandy Review* 30 (September 1962), pp. 50-52.

————, and Panake, John. "P-for-Protesty." *Little Sandy Review* 25 (April 1962), pp. 5-12.

Newman, David. "Return of the Campus Rebel." *Esquire* (September 1961), pp. 14-28.

Ochs, Phil. "Glory Bound." *Mainstream* 16 (August 1963), pp. 34-39.

————. "Have You Heard? The War Is Over." *Village Voice*, November 23, 1967, pp. 4-5.

————. "The Need for Topical Music." *Broadside* 22 (March 1963). pp. 1-2.

————. "An Open Letter from Phil Ochs to Irwin Silber, Paul Wolfe and Joseph R. Levine." *Broadside* 54 (January 1965), pp. 11-12.

————. "Son of 'My Back Pages.'" *Broadside* 57 (April 1965), pp. 12-14.

O'Leary, Tom. "Joan Baez—A Lesser Flop." *World Campus* 11 (December 1967), pp. 3-5, 15.

Paxton, Tom. "Folk Rot." *Sing Out!* 15 (January 1966), pp 103, 105.

"People's Songs—First Year." *People's Songs* 2 (March 1947), pp. 2, 15.

"Pete Seeger's Tour." *Soviet Life* 4 (April 1966), pp. 52-54.

Real, Jere. "Folk Music and Red Tubthumpers." *American Opinion* 7 (December 1964), pp. 19-24.

Reuss, Dick. "So You Want to Be a Folklorist?" *Sing Out!* 15 (November 1965), pp. 40-42.

_____ "Topical Songs from *People's Songs* to *Broadside:* The Changing Times." *Broadside* 55 (February 12, 1965), pp. 4-6.

Reynolds, Malvina. "A Ribbon Bow." *Sing Out!* 13 (Summer 1963), pp. 14-15, 16-17.

Rose, Stephen C. "Bob Dylan as Theologian." *Renewal* (October-December 1965), pp. 4-8.

Sampson, Edward E. "Student Activism and the Decade of Protest." *Journal of Social Issues* 23 (July 1967), pp. 1-33.

Sandperl, Ira. "Peace as a Pitfall." *Institute for the Study of Nonviolence Journal* (November 1967), p. 13.

Seeger, Mike. "A Contemporary Folk Esthetic." *Sing Out!* 16 (February-March 1966), pp. 60-61.

Seeger, Pete. "From Aldermaston to London—They Walked and Sang for Peace." *Sing Out!* 10 (December-January 1960-1961), pp. 14-15.

_____ "Johnny Appleseed, Jr." *Sing Out!* 13 (Summer 1963), pp. 65-66.

_____ "Johnny Appleseed, Jr." *Sing Out!* 13 (December-January 1963-1964), p. 81.

_____ "Johnny Appleseed, Jr." *Sing Out!* 14 (April-May 1961), pp. 89, 91.

_____ "Statement to the Court." *Sing Out!* 11 (April-May 1961), pp. 10-11.

_____ "Strummin' Banjo in North Vietnam." *Saturday Review*, May 13, 1972, pp. 28-29.

_____ "The Theory of Cultural Guerilla Tactics." *Sing Out!* 11 (October-November 1961), pp. 60-61.

_____ "Whatever Happened to Singing in the Unions?" *Sing Out!* 15 (May 1965), pp. 28-31.

_____ "Why Folk Music?" *International Musician* 63 (May 1965), pp. 9-10.

————. "Woody Guthrie and the Gift to Be Simple." *Little Sandy Review* 5 (August 1960), pp. 18-21.

————. "Woody Guthrie: Lessons He Taught Us." *Caravan* 12 (April-May 1959), pp. 14-15.

————. "Woody Guthrie—Some Reminiscences." *Sing Out!* 14 (July 1964), pp. 26-29.

Shaw, Arnold. "The New Folksingers." *Harper's* 229 (November 1964), pp. 33-43.

Silber, Irwin. "Country Joe Unstrung." *Sing Out!* 18 (June 1968), pp. 71-73.

————. "The Cultural Retreat." *Guardian*, December 6, 1969, pp. 17-18.

————. "Fan the Flames." *Sing Out!* 13 (February-March 1963), p. 47.

————. "Fan the Flames." *Sing Out!* 15 (March 1965), pp. 46-48.

————. "Fan the Flames." *Sing Out!* 15 (May 1965), p. 63.

————. "Fan the Flames." *Sing Out!* 15 (July 1965), pp. 69, 71.

————. "Fan the Flames." *Sing Out!* 16 (April-May 1966), pp. 40-41.

————. "Folk Music on Records—Topical Singers." *Sing Out!* 15 (September 1965), pp. 83, 85.

————. "He Sings for Integration." *Sing Out!* 10 (Summer 1960), pp. 4-7.

————. "An Open Letter to Bob Dylan." *Sing Out!* 14 (November 1964), pp. 22-23.

————. "Peggy Seeger—The Voice of America in Folksong." *Sing Out!* 12 (Summer 1962), pp. 4-8.

————. "Woody Guthrie: He Never Sold Out." *National Guardian*, October 14, 1967, p. 10.

Simple, Robert. "Vietnam Critics Stage Sit-Down at White House." *New York Times*, August 7, 1965, p. 3.

"Sing Love, Not Protest." *Time*, February 23, 1968, pp. 92-93.

Somoroff, Bob. "Troublemakers." *Esquire* (September 1963), pp. 78-79.

"To Prison with Love." *Time*, December 11, 1964, p. 60.

Truzzi, Marcello. "Folksongs on the Right." *Sing Out!* 13 (October-November 1963), pp. 51, 53.

"The Un-American Menace." *People's Songs* 2 (December 1947), p. 2.

Wakefield, Don. "I'm Really a Square." *Redbook* 128 (January 1967), pp. 54-55.

Weberman, Alan, and Friesen, Gordon. "Joan Baez and the Bob Dylan Songs." *Broadside* 97 (March 1969), pp. 1-2, 9-10.

Wenner, Jann. "The *Rolling Stone* Interview: Dylan." *Rolling Stone,* November 29, 1969, pp. 23-33.

"What They're Saying." *Sing Out!* 16 (February-March 1966), p. 85.

"What's Happening." *Sing Out!* 15 (November 1965), pp. 6-9.

Willis, Ellen, "The Sound of Bob Dylan." *Commentary* 44 (November 1967), pp. 71-78.

"With a One and a Two and a Wackety-Wack." *Senior Scholastic* 80 (February 21, 1962), pp. 38-39.

Wolfe, Paul. "The New Dylan." *Broadside* 53 (December 20, 1964), pp. 10-12.

"Woody's Boy." *Newsweek,* May 23, 1966, pp. 110, 113.

Young, Israel G. "Frets and Frails." *Sing Out!* 16 (February-March 1966), pp. 63, 65.

Selected Discography

Baez, Joan. *Any Day Now*. Vanguard Records, 1969.

———— *Baptism*. Vanguard Records, 1968.

———— *Blessed Are*. Vanguard Records, 1970.

———— *Come from the Shadows*. A & M Records, 1972.

———— *David's Album*. Vanguard Records, 1969.

———— *The First Ten Years*. Vanguard Records, 1971.

———— *Farewell Angelina*. Vanguard Records, 1965.

———— *Joan*. Vanguard Records, 1967.

———— *Joan Baez*. Vanguard Records, 1960.

———— *The Joan Baez Ballad Book*. Vanguard Records, 1972.

———— *Joan Baez 5*. Vanguard Records, 1964.

———— *Joan Baez in Concert*. Vanguard Records, 1962.

———— *Joan Baez, Volume 2*. Vanguard Records, 1961.

_____ *One Day at a Time*. Vanguard Records, 1961.

_____ *Where Are You Now My Son?* A & M Records, 1973.

Collins, Judy. *Judy Collins Concert*. Elektra Records, 1964.

_____ *Judy Collins 5th Album*. Elektra Records, 1965.

_____ *Judy Collins No. 3*. Elektra Records, 1963.

_____ *Wild Flowers*. Elektra Records, 1967.

Country Joe and the Fish. *I-Feel-Like-I'm-Fixin-to-Die*. Vanguard Records, 1967.

_____ *The Life and Times of Country Joe and the Fish*. Vanguard Records, 1970.

Dylan, Bob. *Another Side of Bob Dylan*. Columbia Records, 1964.

_____ *Blonde on Blonde*. Columbia Records, 1966.

_____ *Bob Dylan*. Columbia Records, 1962.

_____ *Bob Dylan's Greatest Hits*. Columbia Records, 1967.

_____ *Bob Dylan's Greatest Hits, Volume 2*. Columbia Records, 1969.

_____ *Bringing It All Back Home*. Columbia Records, 1965.

_____ *The Freewheelin' Bob Dylan*. Columbia Records, 1963.

_____ *John Wesley Harding*. Columbia Records, 1968.

_____ *Nashville Skyline*. Columbia Records, 1969.

_____ *New Morning*. Columbia Records, 1970.

_____ *Planet Waves*. Asylum Records, 1973.

_____ *Self-Portrait*. Columbia Records, 1970.

_____ *The Times They Are A-Changin'*. Columbia Records, 1964.

The Folksong Tradition. Tradition Records, 1960.

Folksong 65. Elektra Records, 1965.

Gibson, Bob. *Yes I See*. Elektra Records, 1961.

_____, and Camp, Bob. *Gibson and Camp at the Gate of Horn*. Elektra Records, 1962.

Greatest Songs of Woody Guthrie. Vanguard Records, 1970.

Guthrie, Arlo. *Alice's Restaurant*. Reprise Records, 1967.

Guthrie, Woody. *Ballads of Sacco and Vanzetti*. Folkway Records, 1960.

_____ *Bound for Glory*. Folkway Records, n.d.

_____ *Dustbowl Ballads*. RCA Records, 1964.

_____ *The Legendary Woody Guthrie*. Stinson Records, 1967.

_____ *Woody Guthrie Library of Congress Recordings*. Elektra Records, 1964.

Haggard, Merle. *The Best of the Best of Merle Haggard*. Capitol Records, 1972.

Hardin, Tim. *Tim Hardin 1*. Verve/Forecast Records, n.d.

Ian, Janis. *For All the Seasons of Your Mind*. Verve/Forecast Records, 1968.

———— *Janis Ian*. Verve/Forecast Records, 1967.

———— *The Secret Life of J. Eddy Fink*. Verve/Forecast Records, 1969.

Jan and Dean. *Folk 'N Roll*. Liberty Records, 1965.

Jim and Jean. *Changes*. Verve/Forecast Records, 1968.

Kingston Trio. *Children of the Morning*. Capitol Records, 1966.

———— *Time to Think*. Capitol Records, 1964.

La Farge, Peter. *On the Warpath*. Folkways Records, 1965.

Lavender Jane. *Lavender Jane Loves Women*. Women's Music Network, 1974.

The March on Washington, August 28, 1963. Council For United Civil Rights Leadership Record, 1963.

Masten, Ric. *Twelve String Sermons*. Mastenville Records, 1968.

Mitchell, Chad. *Reflecting*. Mercury Records, 1966.

———— *The Slightly Irreverent Mitchell Trio*. Mercury Records, 1967.

———— *Violets of the Dawn*. Mercury Records, 1968.

Mitchell, Joni. *For the Roses*. Asylum Records, 1972.

———— *Ladies of the Canyon*. Elektra Records, 1968.

New Lost City Ramblers, *Songs from the Depression*. Folkways Records, 1961.

Newman, Randy. *Sail Away*. Reprise Records, 1972.

Newport Broadside. Vanguard Records, 1963.

Ochs, Phil. *All the News That's Fit to Sing*. Elektra Records. 1964.

———— *I Ain't Marching Anymore*. Elektra Records, 1965.

———— *Phil Ochs' Greatest Hits*. A & M Records, 1970.

———— *Phil Ochs in Concert*. Elektra Records, 1966.

———— *Pleasures of the Harbor*. Elektra Records, 1967.

———— *Rehearsals for Retirement*. A & M Records, 1969.

———— *Tape from California*. Elektra Records, 1968.

Odetta. *Ballad for Americans*. Vanguard Records, 1965.

———— *Odetta Sings Dylan*. RCA Victor, 1965.

Oglesby, Carl. *Carl Oglesby*. Vanguard Records, 1967.

Paxton, Tom. *Ain't That News*. Elektra Records, 1965.

_____ *Peace Will Come*. Reprise Records, 1972.

_____ *Ramblin' Boy*. Elektra Records, 1964.

_____ *Tom Paxton 5*. Elektra Records, 1970.

Previn, Dory. *Dory Previn—Live at Carnegie Hall*. United Artists Records, 1973.

Prine, John. *John Prine*. Atlantic Records, 1971.

Reynolds, Malvina. *Malvina Reynolds Sings the Truth*. Columbia Records, 1966.

Sainte-Marie, Buffy. *It's My Way*. Vanguard Records, 1964.

_____ *Little Wheels Spin and Spin*. Vanguard Records, 1966.

_____ *Moonshot*. Vanguard Records, 1972.

_____ *Quiet Places*. Vanguard Records, 1973.

Seeger, Pete. *American Industrial Ballads*. Folkway Records, n.d.

_____ *Dangerous Songs*. Columbia Records, 1966.

_____ *Gazette, Volume I*. Folkway Records, 1958.

_____ *God Bless the Grass*. Columbia Records, 1966.

_____ *I Can See a New Day*. Columbia Records. 1964.

_____ *Young vs. Old*. Columbia Records, 1970.

_____ *Waist Deep in the Big Muddy*. Columbia Records, 1963.

_____ *With Voices Together We Sing*. Folkways Records, n.d.

Simon and Garfunkel. *Wednesday Morning, 3 A.M.* Columbia Records, 1964.

This Land Is Your Land: Songs of Social Justice. United Autoworkers, 1964.

Time Is Running Out. Broadside Records, 1970.

Virgo Rising: The Once and Future Woman. Thunderbird Records, 1972.

Weissman, Dick. *The Things That Trouble My Mind*. Capitol Records, 1965.

Index

A & M Records, 77
Adnopoz, Elliott, 56
Agnew, Spiro, 32, 145
"Alan Burke Show," 88
All the News That's Fit to Sing, 67
Almanac Singers, 8
Alternate media, x
American Communist Party, 10
American Folksongs of Protest, 59
American Labor Party, 10
Anarchists, 4
Antiestablishment, 62
Antioch College, 98
Asch, Moe, 48

Baez, Joan
    atmosphere of her concerts, 18
    and civil rights, 86
    compared to other protest singers, 151
    criticism of, 97
    as cultural hero, 98-99
    early life, 84-85
    guest on TV talk shows, 88-89
    marriage to David Harris, 87
    musical style, 92-96
    and pacifism, 86-87, 90-91
    as tax resister, 83
Beatles, the, 32, 111
Beatniks, 57, 105
Berkeley Free Speech Movement, 68, 86, 99
Bettelheim, Bruno, 64
Bikel, Theo, 11, 144

Bilbo, Theodore, 9
Black power, 97
"Blowin' in the Wind," 20, 66, 101, 107, 114
Boorstin, Daniel, xv-xvi
Born to Win, 58
Bound for Glory, 8, 44, 53, 56, 58, 60
Bowie, David, 139
Brazier, Richard, 5
Broadside, 20, 36, 65-66, 70, 79, 115, 126, 138
Bromberg, David, 79

Campbell, Glen, 35
Campus Crusade for Christ, 33
Capitalism, 34-35
Capp, Al, 97
Cash, Johnny, 93, 125
Castro, Fidel, 68, 73
Chad Mitchell Trio, 13
Chaplin, Ralph, 4, 6
Chavez, Cesar, 60, 99
Chicago Seven, 81
Christian Crusade, 18, 140
"Christian World Liberation Front," 28
Civil rights movement, 13, 20
Clayton, Paul, 107
Cohen, Leonard, 35, 140
College students
    as audience for protest singers, 15
    musical tastes of, 12
    in 1960s compared to 1950s, xix, 37-38
Collier, Jeremy, 19
Collins, Judy, 13, 61, 90, 142
Columbia River Project, 8
Communism, 10-11, 18, 32
Congress of Industrial Organizations (CIO), 6
Cooper, Alice, 140
Cooper, James Fenimore, xvii
Counter culture, 31, 133-34
Counterattack, 10
"The Crucifixion," 73, 81
Cultural heroes
    artists as, xvii-xviii
    compared to celebrities, xvi-xvii
    protest singers as, 49-50, 98-99, 133, 146-48
    traditional, xvi

Daily Worker, 47, 53
"David Frost Show," 89
Davis, Rennie, 145
Daybreak, 91, 94, 119
Dean, James, 78, 81, 104
Dellinger, Dave, 76
Denisoff, R. Serge, viii, 59
Dewey, Thomas, 51
"Dick Cavett Show," 88
Donovan (Leitch), 74, 143
Doors, the, 75
"Draft Dodger Rag," 68
Drugs, 32, 97, 132
Dylan, Bob
    appealed to by Baez, 95
    compared to Baez, 96
    compared to various protest singers, 151
    criticized by Ochs, 75
    defended by Ochs, 70-71
    defends Pete Seeger, 14-15
    early life, 102-6
    evolution of his music, 112-26
    as existential hero, 147

existential stress of, 16
influence of Guthrie, 56
and Judaism, 103
as model for other protest singers, 66
and New York folk scene, 107-8
personal philosophy, 130-32
on Phil Ochs, 63
and protest song revival, 150
social effect, 133-34
symbolism of songs, 129
turns away from protest music, 23-24, 109-10, 116-18

"Ed Sullivan Show," 114
Edwards, Jonathan, 17
Electric music, 24, 77
Elektra Records, 67, 75, 77
Elliott, Jack, 48, 56, 65
Ellis, Havelock, 36
Emerson, Ralph Waldo, 58
Evers, Medgar, 81

Fariña, Mimi, 95
Fariña, Richard, 93, 114
Federal Arts Project, 8, 47-48
Folk music
 and college students, 12-13
 defined, xiii-xvi
 favorable images of, xv, xvi
 as music of the masses, 146
 and the political left, xiv, 10-11, 14

as topical songs, 4
Folk music revival, 20, 141-42, 149
Folk-rock, 15, 21, 23, 33, 110, 139-40
Folkniks, 13, 57
Fonda, Jane, xviii
Forman, Jim, 117
Friesen, Gordon, 59, 123, 126, 142
Fugs, the, 140
Fundamentalism, 141

Gandhi, Mahatma, 93, 97, 99
Geer, Will, 46
Gerde's Folk-City, 107
Gibson, Bob, 65
Gilbert, Ronnie, 48
Ginsberg, Allen, 61, 102
Gleason, Ralph, 114, 126, 147
Glover, Jim, 65
"The Gol-dern Red," 9
Goldberg, Steven, 124
Goldwater, Barry, 64
Goodman, Paul, 38
Grapes of Wrath, 47, 54
Greenblatt, Marjorie Mazia, 48
Greenway, John, 59
Greenwich Village, 65, 106-7
Guest, Edgar, 125
Guevara, Che, 52
Guthrie, Arlo, 50, 56, 142
Guthrie, Charles, 44
Guthrie, Nora, 44
Guthrie, Woody
 compared to Abraham Lincoln, 57
 compared to other protest singers, 151
 as cultural hero, 49-50

declining influence, 141, 143
defends protest songs, 25
drifts around country, 46-47
early life, 44-46
evaluations of, 58-62
influence on Dylan, 105
instrumental ability, 23
as model, 7-8, 12, 56
and New York folk revival, 48
and political left, 47-48, 52-53

Haggard, Merle, 36
Halberstram, David, 147
Haley, Bill, 105
Hammond, John, 107
"A Hard Rain's A-Gonna Fall," 114
Hardin, Tim, 35, 74, 143
Harris, David, xvii, 27, 84, 86-87, 89, 91
Hawthorne, Nathaniel, xvii
Hayden, Tom, 76, 103, 145
Hays, Lee, 48
Hellerman, Fred, 48
Hentoff, Nat, 72, 116, 121
"Here's to the Government of Richard Nixon," 79
Herzog, Arthur, 148
Hester, Carolyn, xv, 107
Hill, Joe, 4, 50, 76, 81
Hippies, 130
Holzman, Jac, 75
Hootenanny, 14
Hoover, Herbert, 52
House Un-American Activities Committee, 10, 14

Houston, Cisco, 48
Huntington's chorea, 45, 49

"I Ain't Marching Anymore," 67, 72, 76
Ian, Janis, 18, 143
Ifshin, David, 78
Institute for the Study of Nonviolence, 83, 90
International Workers of the World (IWW), 4
"It Isn't Nice," 90
Ives, Burl, 50

Jackson, Andrew, 58
Jackson, George, 126
Jazz, 12
Jefferson Airplane, the, 138, 140
Jesus, 81
Jim and Jean, 65
Joan of Arc, 99
John Wesley Harding, 122-23
Johnson, Lyndon, 35, 74
Joplin, Janis, 95

Kai-shek, Chiang, 68
Kennedy, John F., 39, 68, 81, 83, 98
Kerouac, Jack, 102, 105
King, Martin Luther, 11, 13, 20, 66, 97, 99
Kingston Trio, 13, 50
Ku Klux Klan, 35
Kunen, James Simon, 21, 34, 144

Labor songs, 5-7
Lampell, Millard, 59
Landau, Jon, 124
Lasch, Christopher, xix, 81
Leadbelly
(Huddie Ledbetter), 92

Leary, Timothy, 19
Lees, Gene, xiii
Lennon, John, 34, 95
"Les Crane Show," 88, 99
Lester, Julius, 149
Lewis, Sinclair, 103
Liberals, 13, 28, 69, 81
Lincoln, Abraham, 57
Linkletter, Art, 32
"Links on the Chain," 67
"Little Red Songbook," 5-6
Little, Richard, 105
Little Sandy Review, 55, 92, 138
Lomax, Alan, 47
"Love Me I'm a Liberal," 69
Love Story, 138
Lowndes, Sarah, 110-11

McCarthy, Eugene, 76
McCarthy, Joe, 10-11
McCartney, Paul, 34
McDonald, Country Joe, 29, 38, 51
McGovern, George, 81, 145
McGuinn, Roger, 18, 20
McKuen, Rod, 125
McLean, Don, 82
McLuhan, Marshall, xviii, 37-38, 98, 102, 127
Main Street, 103
Malcolm X, 99
Manson, Charlie, 78
"March on Washington," 86
Marcuse, Herbert, 104
Marsh, Lou, 81
Martyrs, 81-83
Marxism, 31-32, 133, 141
Masten, Ric, 22
MC5, 140
Melanie, 144
Mercouri, Melina, 95
Mills, C. Wright, 31

Mitchell, Joni, 35, 138, 140, 143
Monroe, Marilyn, xvii
Monterey Folk Festival, 108
"My Back Pages," 24, 109, 133

Nader, Ralph, 99
Nashville (Tennessee), 94, 112
National States Rights Party, 36
Nationalism, 84, 91, 95
Nelson, Paul, xiv, 55, 125
New Deal's Federal Arts Projects, 8, 54
New Left, 67, 73, 78-79, 80, 131
"New radicalism," xix, 31
Newman, Randy, 82
Newport Folk Festival, 24, 55, 85, 108, 110
Nico and the Velvet Underground, 139
Nixon, Richard, 79, 145
Noebel, David, 18, 31, 52, 97, 141
Nonviolence, 85-86, 90-91, 95
North Vietnam, 95

Ochs, Phil
    as agitator, 63
    defends protest songs, 24
    on Dylan, 70-71, 75
    early life, 64-65
    as martyr, 81-82
    musical decline, 78-80
    and New Left, 68-70, 73-74, 76
    and New York folk scene, 66-67
Okun, Milton, 58

Pacifism, 67, 85-86, 90-91
Panake, John, xiv
Pauling, Linus, 148
Paxton, Tom, xi, 53, 61, 107
People's Daily World, 46-47, 53
People's Songs, 8, 10-12, 48
Peter, Paul, and Mary, 13, 15, 86
Picasso, Pablo, xix, 99
Plato, xix, 19
Pope, Alexander, 18
Popular music
    dominated by rock music, 139
    and drugs, 32-33
    major categories of, xiv-xv
    new stress on lyrics, 20, 138
    and protest music, 13, 33
Presley, Elvis, 78, 105
Progressive Party, 10, 48
"The Protest Biz," 22
Protest singers
    and college audience, 12
    and commercialism, 35-36
    as cultural heroes, ix, xvi-xviii, 149-51
    as general authorities, 148
    older compared to younger, 11
    as radical influences, 28-30
    as revivalists, 17-18, 25
    as social rebels, 146-47
    stereotyped, 15-16
Protest songs
    commercial aspects of, 22-23
    compared to Vietnamese protest songs, 37
    as conservative force, 35-36
    as dangerous, 18-19
    decline, 142-43
    evolution of, 3-15
    examples of conscience, 39
    Guthrie-Seeger tradition in, 141-42
    haziness of, 15-16, 137-38
    and International Workers of the World, 4-6
    and Marxist ideology, 31-32
    Negro spirituals as, 4
    and revivalism, 17-18, 25
    as substitute for action, 34
    swallowed up by rock music, 139
    symbol of an era, 25
    and unions, 3-6
Procul Harum, 139

Radicals, 27-28, 31, 38
Red-baiting, 10
Red Channels, 11
Reuss, Dick, xiv
Reynolds, Malvina, 29, 70, 90, 93
Rock concerts, 140
Rock music, 12, 21, 139-40
Rolling Stone, 131, 139
Rolling Stones, 30, 111, 138
Rotolo, Suze, 107, 109
Roxon, Lillian, 60
Rubin, Jerry, 61, 64, 76, 78, 103, 145

SANE Emergency Rally, 86
"Saigon Bride," 87
St. Marie, Buffy, 37
Sandperl, Ira, 90
Sartre, Jean-Paul, 125
Scaduto, Anthony, 71
Schweitzer, Albert, 99
Seeger, Pete
   and Almanac Singers, 8
   Baez dedicates song to, 92
   as cultural guerilla, 15
   on decline of protest music, 149
   on difference between writer and performer, 128
   and Guthrie, 47, 53
   and HUAC, 14
   on limitations of protest songs, 39
   as model for younger singers, xi, 14, 66
   optimistic about protest music, 11, 19
   and People's Songs, 8-9
   and the Weavers, 12
Segal, Erich, 138
Shelton, Bob, 75, 107
Siegel, Jules, 122
Silber, Irwin, 35, 52, 58, 70, 115, 139, 141
Simon, Paul, 16, 138, 142
Sing Out!, 10, 20, 131, 139
Slick, Grace, 140
"Song to Woody," 108
Smith, Howard K., 88
"Solidarity Forever," 6
Spock, Benjamin, 148
Stevens, Cat, 140
Stowe, Harriet Beecher, xvii

Streisand, Barbra, 96
Student activism, 145
Students for a Democratic Society (SDS), 63, 69, 73
Syndicalists, 4

"Talking John Birch Society Blues," 108
Tarantula, 127
Terry, Blind Sonny, 48
Thoreau, Henry, 29, 34, 49, 82, 104
"The Times They Are A-Changin'," 66, 101
Tin Pan Alley songs, xiv
Truman, Harry, 121
Truth, Sojourner, 15
Tse-tung, Mao, 68

Union songs, 5-7
Unions, 6-7, 11, 46, 67
United Mine Workers, 6
United Nations, 97
University of Illinois, 92
University of Minnesota, 106
Van Ronk, Dave, 65, 107
Vanguard Records, 75, 85
Viet Cong, 37, 73
The Vietnam Songbook, 23
Vietnam war, 73-74, 84, 86-87, 124, 129

Wald, George, 148
Wallace, Henry, 9, 48
"The War Is Over," 76
Ward, Ed, 126
Watson, Doc, 79
"We Shall Overcome," 20, 93
Weavers, 12, 48
Weberman, Alan, 93, 123
Welch, Raquel, 79

West, Don, 72
"What Have They Done to the Rain," 87, 93
White Panther Party, 140
Whitman, Walt, 7, 16, 51
Williams, Paul, 125
"With God on Our Side," 93, 108
Wolfe, Paul, 71, 115
Woman's liberation, 36, 97-98, 145

Woodstock Music Festival, 92
Worthy, William, 81

Yarrow, Peter, 19
Yippies, 63, 74, 76
Young, Israel, 118

Zappa, Frank, ix, 29, 96
Zen Buddhism, xiv
Zimmerman, Abe, 102
Zimmerman, Robert, 102, 106